THIRTEENTH NIGHT
&
A SHORT SHARP SHOCK!

Published alongside the first production of *Thirteenth Night* by the Royal Shakespeare Company, this is a double volume of two intensely topical yet very different plays. They display two contrasting approaches to political playwriting by Howard Brenton, whose recent work has included *The Romans in Britain* and a translation of Brecht's *Galileo,* both staged by the National Theatre.

Thirteenth Night is 'a dream play', skilfully reworking Shakespearian themes into a political thriller in which a British Stalin (Jack Beaty), having despatched the over-moderate Prime Minister (Bill Dunn), himself becomes a murderous tyrant.

The second play, *A Short Sharp Shock!,* written with Tony Howard, is an outright anti-Thatcherite polemic, which attracted enormous attention – and packed houses – in the summer of 1980.

by Howard Brenton

THE CHURCHILL PLAY
EPSOM DOWNS
MAGNIFICENCE
PLAYS FOR THE POOR THEATRE
(The Saliva Milkshake, Christie in Love, Gum and Goo, Heads,
   The Education of Skinny Spew)
THE ROMANS IN BRITAIN
SORE THROATS & SONNETS OF LOVE AND OPPOSITION
WEAPONS OF HAPPINESS

with David Hare
BRASSNECK

translation
THE LIFE OF GALILEO by Bertolt Brecht

THIRTEENTH NIGHT

by

HOWARD BRENTON

&

A SHORT SHARP SHOCK!

by

HOWARD BRENTON

and

TONY HOWARD

A Methuen New Theatrescript
Eyre Methuen · London

First published in 1981 by Eyre Methuen Ltd, 11 New Fetter Lane, London EC4P 4EE
Thirteenth Night © 1981 by Howard Brenton
A Short Sharp Shock! © 1981 by Howard Brenton and Tony Howard
Printed in Great Britain by Expression Printers Ltd, London N7

ISBN 0 413 48500 5

THIRTEENTH NIGHT

A dream play

To Marion and George

Thirteenth Night was first presented by the Royal Shakespeare Company at the Warehouse, London on 2 July 1981, with the following cast:

JACK BEATY	Michael Pennington
JENNY GAZE	Domini Blythe
BERNARD FEAST	John Bowe
BILL DUNN	David Waller
HENRY MURGATROYD	Derek Godfrey
ROSS	Paul Webster
ROSE	Avril Clark
CYGNA	Shelagh Stephenson
JOAN	Sara Mason

FEAST doubles as an AMBASSADOR, DUNN and MURGATROYD as MURDERERS, ROSE, CYGNA and JOAN as C.I.A. AGENTS.

Directed by Barry Kyle
Designed by Bob Crowley
Music by Nick Bicât
Lighting by Leo Leibovici

N.B. This is the text of the play on the first day of rehearsal.

Induction

Night. A South London street.
A PUBLICAN'S VOICE, *off-stage.*

VOICE: Time, time, come on everyone.

JACK BEATY *and* JENNY GAZE
come on.

BEATY: Good meeting.

GAZE: Think so?

BEATY: The issues were very sharp.

GAZE: Oh in the pub afterwards. Very
sharp. The sound of Labour Party
democracy – breaking glass and men's
voices raised at closing time.

BEATY: Still. All shall be well and all
manner of things shall be well. Can we go
to your place tonight, Jenny?

They stare at each other.

GAZE: Why?

BEATY: She's – going to ring tonight.

GAZE: 'She' meaning your wife.

BEATY: I can't face another of those calls.
Three hour calls. Not after a Labour
Party Ward Meeting. Human flesh is
human flesh.

GAZE: 'Human flesh' meaning 'Male
flesh?'

BEATY: We can't be there – with her on
the 'phone –

GAZE: Take it off the hook –

BEATY: She'd ring all night, just to listen
to the engaged tone – come the dawn, get
the GPO to make that buzzing noise –
please.

BERNARD FEAST *comes on.*

FEAST: Better get a taxi. Bill's well away.

BEATY: All right Bernard.

FEAST: We going to talk later tonight?

BEATY: Yes – yes –

FEAST: I'll give a hand with Bill.

FEAST *goes off.*

BEATY: God –

GAZE: Why does every Ward Meeting end
up with our Chairperson drunk?

BEATY: Water the grass-roots. Can I?

Come back?

GAZE: You're going to talk to Bernard.

BEATY: Do that at your place. Or –

GAZE: Doesn't it strike you as sickening, a
little bit sickening – working for a
Socialist Britain when we can't even run a
little love affair? I mean – have we the
right to call for a New Social Order when
we can't even keep our own bodies under
control?

BEATY: Dark thoughts, Jen! (*Low:*) I
want love.

GAZE (*low*): Oh we all want love.

BILL DUNN, *supported by* HENRY
MURGATROYD *and* FEAST, *comes
on.* ROSS *follows and walks a distance
away.*

DUNN: In 1937 my old Dad – said he were
going out for a walk. Tea-time it were.
Three year he were gone and not a word!
Bugger had enlisted for 'International
Brigade in 'Spanish Civil War! My old
Dad –

MURGATROYD: Yes Bill, we know the
story –

FEAST: Not a postcard –

MURGATROYD: } Or an 'and-grenade –
DUNN:

FEAST: Someone getting a taxi?

FEAST *wanders off,* MURGATROYD
keeping DUNN *upright.*

ROSS: Are you and Bernard meeting
tonight?

BEATY (*looking at* JENNY): Don't know.
Yes.

ROSS: We need two more Wards to get the
Selection Committee our way. That
means a lot of telephone calls, tonight.

BEATY: We're only a piddling little caucus
in a Ward Party – can't we sleep?

ROSS (*low*): It matters!

BEATY (*low*): I know it matters!

GAZE: You can come to my place.

BEATY: Thanks, love.

GAZE: We must get rid of our resident
right-wing Labour pig of an MP, must we
not. (*She looks away.*)

DUNN: Fixing it up are you? Between you? Carving it up?

FEAST: Jack, over the street.

> FEAST, BEATY, GAZE *and* ROSS *staring across the street.*

DUNN: You're a bloody menace, all of you. Tell you what your trouble is – anal fixation. That were Clem Attlee's trouble. And Robespierre's.

MURGATROYD: Don't quite get the connection there, Bill.

DUNN: Too precise. Turd counters, the lot of you.

FEAST: Those thugs who were in the other bar.

ROSS: I know them.

FEAST: Get that taxi –

DUNN: Bloody paperback Marxists. Ah no no, the young. Dialectically engaged. I love to see 'em scrum.

MURGATROYD: He's going to throw up.

DUNN: Just hold me while I breathe!

MURGATROYD: Help me hold him –

ROSS: Here they come.

MURGATROYD: Tell you what Jack, Jenny –

> ROSS, *taking out a length of piping.*

FEAST: Taxi, there's got to be a taxi –

ROSS: Fascists.

DUNN: If a socialist party really came t'power in Britain, not Labour Party, real Socialist Party – what would it face? Eh? Jack? Jenny? You come to power tomorrow, prison notebooks o' Antonio Gramsci and all – what do you do eh?

> *They all stare. They take a step back.* DUNN *lurches forward.*

DUNN: Nazis? Blackshirts? Get 'em all –

> *As if the attackers are a few feet away, running toward them. Then* GAZE *is hit, she goes down.*

BEATY: Jenny –

> *He moves towards* GAZE *and goes down.*

FEAST: Scum!

DUNN: Get 'em –

MURGATROYD: Bill don't –

DUNN: Get 'em all!

> ROSS, *his piping coming down on a head.* *Blackout.* *The sound of a fight, then cut off.*

> *Silence.*

Scene One

BEATY, *alone on the ground.*
From a dreamscape to the Central Hall,
Westminster.

BEATY: Get 'em all, get 'em all.

I'll put on my gloves, not to make the
piano dirty, Mum.

Ha!

He sits up.

I still get a nightmare. I am a concert
pianist, in black tails, white bow-tie, shiny
black dress shoes. Hands manicured and
flexed I walk from my dressing-room
alone, along the corridor. I listen to my
breath. Then I'm on the platform.
Wham! The audience a mountainside of
humanity, raging for music. The
orchestra a band of brilliant men and
women, disciplined and honed, all their
eyes blue. And on the conductor's
podium, his baton one mile long – why,
Karl Marx. I flip the tails of my dress suit.
Sit upon the stool. Caress my knuckles
over the keys. It's the big one! The great
concerto! Karl's baton moves, the tip a
star dancing among the constellations!
The orchestra crashes in, the great chords
ascend – intolerable excitement – my
ribcage burns – Karl nods to me – my
entrance – I raise my hands like hawks to
bring them down, and –

I remember. I can't play the piano.

It's a ghastly mistake, why am I here – I
can't play, I –

And it's frozen, the moment, I – wake up.

He scrambles away wiping his face with a
handkerchief. The buzz of a three-
thousand-strong crowd. A batch of
microphones rises from the stage. He turns
towards them.

So, how long can I go on grinding out the
notes of a music I can't believe in? Who is
playing for whom? Who is dancing?

Comrades. After decades of dereliction.
Of the working class on right-wing
adventures at the ballot-box. Of the
Labour Movement mis-led, split, done
down by petit-bourgeois politicians,
messing their pants with fear at what real
socialist policies would mean to them.
Personally. To their cosy little world, the
cat's cradle of how Government right or
centre or left has always worked in this
country. The secret deal. In the leather
armchairs of London clubs, over bone
china in the House of Commons tea-
room, everyone with their tongue in the
right ear and everyone with a seat on the
board of a City bank being kept warm. No
messy, grass-roots democracy. Just
leaders in *The Times* and *Daily Mail,*
telling them what the country thinks.

Well, we've struck a blow at that. Go to
Heathrow Airport these days. See what
fabulous refugees are on the wing to the
swamps of Florida.

I am proud to serve in a Government
which is driving so many of our so-called
'powerful people' abroad.

But. The rub. But.

We have been in power twelve months.
And I do not yet know whether we really
do mean what we say. Let alone if we are
going to do – what we say.

A 'Great Agitation' has put us in power.
At last a majority of the electorate is
against Death. Which is a wonderful
thing. More, they are against Nuclear
Death. Which is a very wonderful thing.
It's taken a long time, but wonderful. We
are to disarm our nuclear forces,
unilaterally. The electorate says we are,
the Cabinet says we are, even the Prime
Minister says we are.

But are we? Abandon nuclear weapons
and we leave the Western world. And the
Western world leaves us. I mean, of
course, American money. But since half
our country is owned by America we
would be left a bleeding corpse on the
shore of Northern Europe. Right! The
only course, nationalise American assets.
And get poorer. For the cost of
international sanity will be poverty.
Which can only be made tolerable by a
new equity. A new social justice – the
policies we have all striven for. With new
friends abroad. For socialism in this
country will, like it or not, drive us to our
only moral place in the world. Britain
must join the Third World. New friends.
And a new enemy. America.

A roar from the crowd. Then BEATY,
low:

I have a kind of fear. That – we don't have

the politics to do it. That it is going to be so troublesome, the strain, the subversion against us, the terrible strain cannot be born by Government as we know it. That we need a new democracy, new forms, a politics to end politics.

For if we do not take a stand from which there is no going back – once and for all –

We –

He freezes.

Will –

Be –

Lost –

A silence. Then the crowd very loud and a blackout.

Scene Two

A bunker beneath Whitehall.
BILL DUNN *and* HENRY
MURGATROYD. MURGATROYD
holds a red telephone.

DUNN: How bad is it?

MURGATROYD *listens to the telephone then replaces the receiver. He is silent.*

Come on. How many shop windows smashed? Cars turned over? Slogans daubed?

(*To himself*:) Daubed.

MURGATROYD: The Commissioner says it's only a matter of time before someone gets killed.

DUNN: Hunh.

MURGATROYD: Ninety minutes since the meeting broke up. Flowed out of Central Hall, over Parliament Square. Whitehall, red paint on the lions in Trafalgar Square –

DUNN: Par for the course –

MURGATROYD: Eighty-four policemen have been injured. One hundred and twelve arrests, so far. Grosvenor Square is jammed. The crowd wants to burn the American Embassy.

DUNN: Ha! Someone's dream come true, eh?

MURGATROYD: What are you going to do about him, Bill?

A silence.

DUNN: Give us a fag.

MURGATROYD: Given up.

DUNN: Since when?

MURGATROYD: Two days.

DUNN: Hunh! We're two of a kind, Henry. Big, shambolic men who yearn to have tidy minds. S'our destiny to smoke. Ash burning knees of our suits –

MURGATROYD: For Godsake, Bill! On his feet in Westminster Central Hall. TV lights blazing in his hair. Tearing into your leadership –

DUNN: Jack Beaty is hero of the night, all right.

MURGATROYD: Save us from heroes of

the night.

DUNN: Hunh!

DUNN, *patting his suit for cigarettes.*

MURGATROYD: Dismiss him.

DUNN *signs and sags.*

From the Cabinet. It's dissension! It's disloyalty! It's wild, it's adventurism, it's – mess. You know what Lenin called it – infantile disorders.

DUNN: Lenin called many things many things, according to temperature o' water.

MURGATROYD: 'Politics is about power'

DUNN: Aye aye –

MURGATROYD: ⎤ 'Who does what and
DUNN: ⎦ to whom.'

DUNN: Don't let's end up quoting Lenin at each other, not at this hour o' night. That would really be 'bloody end. I can handle Jack Beaty. An idealist is Jack.

MURGATROYD: And like all idealists, a menace. They get too many people singing loony tunes.

DUNN: Party loves it, though. Pressure from below. That not what we want, what we slobber for?

MURGATROYD: The mob up there tonight, baying at the American Embassy, that's not pressure, working-class pressure for social justice. That's just – steam. Come the dawn, a bit of damp on the pavement.

DUNN: Ay aye.

The telephone rings.

I could do with a drink.

MURGATROYD: And a havana cigar?

He lifts the telephone.

You know what this place is, down here?

He puts the telephone to his ear.

DUNN: I know I know. Churchill's War Room. Ha! Look at me. Prime Minister o' first elected Marxist Government in England's green and pleasant, hiding underground.

Someone's got to look at me, I don't dare. A political heavy, jerking about – pulled by the strings of his dilemma. What is leadership? What is a vanguard?

Ha! Thank you, great public, you great electoral roll. Years you elect governments of right-wing yobbos, or Social Democratic ditherers. Then at the eleventh hour, twenty-third hour, you turn round to me and my brothers and sisters and say – 'Right. You're on. The road to Socialism.'

Well it's too bloody late, it may just be too bloody late. The country's all but stripped bare.

MURGATROYD *replaces the telephone.*

MURGATROYD: Twelve have been killed. There may be more.

The first floor of the American Embassy is blazing.

DUNN: Blazing –

MURGATROYD: On fire.

A silence. Then DUNN *shouts.*

DUNN: Ross! Get in here!

How many of the twelve are policemen?

MURGATROYD: Three. Two uniformed, one Special Branch in the crowd.

ROSS *comes on, unobserved.*

DUNN: Well!

He claps his hands.

Tasty.

He shouts: Ross! Get in here! Oh, you are in here. Got a drink on you, Ross? No you are a teetotal vegetarian. Gentlemen you stink of carrot juice and menthol chewing- gum.

Right.

Public statement. No distancing of my Government from tonight's hoo-ha. 'We're all Red Indians now' – summat like that.

MURGATROYD: We can't –

DUNN (*angrily*): Shut up!

We're old comrades, Henry. But don't try to teach your Grandma to suck eggs.

A silence.

Jack Beaty.

ROSS: The man of the hour.

DUNN: I love the bastard. I want all your best men on him, Ross. Surveillance, everything.

ROSS: Yes.

DUNN: Not that you've not got your electronic eye on all of us already, eh Ross?

Nothing from ROSS.

But I want reports on him, round the clock. First thing every morning, last thing every night. Who he 'phones, who he meets, where he scratches himself. Then – we'll get tonight's little holiday back to earth. Back into 'politics we know, eh Gentlemen?

He laughs.

Prime Minister's bunker under the Admiralty? Churchill's War Room? Break open a good rich London sewer. Flood the place.

(*Angrily*:) I'm sick of being a leader who believes in no more leadership.

Scene Three

An underground car-park. ROSE *and* CYGNA.

ROSE: Where have you been?

CYGNA: One more room, one more meeting. You?

ROSE: Watching pigs get stuck.

CYGNA: Too many agendas. Too many points of order glittering like razor blades.

ROSE: How can we keep the richness of dreams, yet be fully awake?

ROSE *laughs.*

CYGNA: Not, I begin to think, in endless meetings. Resolutions, referrals back. And nothing changed.

ROSE: You're right of course. Everything is changed and nothing is changed. 'A People's Government' elected but where are the people? Power still flows along the wires of late-night telephones.

CYGNA: And in men's voices.

ROSE: Oh –

ROSE *holds her face.*

CYGNA: Are you all right?

ROSE: I think there's glass in my eye.

CYGNA: Get to a hospital.

ROSE: There'll be a policeman on every ward tonight. Let it melt, into the blood-stream.

JOAN *runs on.*

JOAN: Beaty's coming.

ROSE: The bloody man.

CYGNA: Wind him up. Set him going.

JOAN: We must do it right. We must remember –

ROSE: Sh!

JACK BEATY *and* BERNARD FEAST *come on.*

FEAST: Where are the security guards?

BEATY: Securing a good night out. Will the police police themselves? No.

BEATY *stops.*

FEAST: Let's get to the car.

BEATY: Bernard. Twelve dead. And the Embassy on fire –

FEAST: We'll get hard news on the 'phone, in the car –

BEATY: But think.

He holds FEAST back.

If the American Ambassador is one of the twelve.

FEAST: We don't know that.

BEATY: But that will be my doing, tonight. Ha! Every public speaker dreams of making a riot, just once in his life. Of the audience – getting up – and actually doing what has been said. Eh?

It's coming over me. A rosy glow. I feel sick.

FEAST: Beaty, pull yourself together.

BEATY retches. FEAST looks about them, nervously.

For godsake –

BEATY: I see his body. In front of me. On a little trolley. On little rubber wheels, soundless. I'll push it about in front of me.

FEAST: We don't know it's happened. It's just rumour, in the crowds.

BEATY: But don't you understand – I want it to have happened? Part of me does.

He laughs.

The rhetorician, dreaming of reality.

And haven't you always said – America will no more allow Britain to be independent and socialist than Russia allowed Czechoslovakia to be independent – and socialist.

FEAST: You're whirling. You're – we'll talk in the car.

He pulls BEATY's arms. BEATY looks around him.

ROSE, CYGNA and JOAN *in the shadows.*

ROSE: Comrade Minister. Why do you park your car underground?

A silence.

For crying out loud –

FEAST, *pulling out a gun.*

BEATY (*to* FEAST): No!

(*Into the dark:*) Who are you?

ROSE: Women with a question.

BEATY: What?

CYGNA: Is the revolution won or lost, Jack Beaty?

FEAST: I know what this is. Don't stand and listen to this.

BEATY: Sh!

JOAN: Go everywhere with your dog, Beaty?

BEATY: We all need dogs these days, comrade. If you value your life, guard it like an off-licence.

FEAST (*low*): Thank you. Thank you very much.

BEATY (*low*): Bernard, no.

(*A silence. Then* BEATY, *aloud:*) Well? Are you going to show yourselves?

FEAST: They're loonies, Jack, I know the tone.

BEATY: Who is a loony and who is not, when it comes to politics?

FEAST: Have nothing to do with them.

ROSE: What is that man afraid of?

CYGNA: People in the streets.

JOAN: They'll come into the streets for you, Jack Beaty.

CYGNA: They did tonight.

JOAN: And burned down a big eagle.

FEAST: Nothing Beaty said tonight sanctions the fire at the American Embassy. Or has anything to do with that.

You Anarchos! Ultras, dreamers. After years we have an elected Socialist Government in this country. But will you work for it? Keep it to its policies, its duty to the working class? Oh no. You are too pure in mind. When you can't bend the real world into Paradise, you want to smash it. For you it's all or nothing. The Garden of Eden or a planet of dust.

ROSE: What, in Paris, made De Gaulle leave for Germany by helicopter? What, in Prague, made Stalin piss in his grave? What, in Teheran, broke the Shah? A new politics.

JOAN: The politics to end politics.

BEATY (*to* FEAST): God! I said that.

CYGNA: Then live it.

ROSE: The road from Evil to Good is worse than Evil.

JOAN: But what decent man or woman dare not go down the road to good?

FEAST (*to* BEATY): Another quote from your collected works?

ROSE: You're the man, Beaty.

BEATY: A saint? Don't we know by now all saints are killers?

ROSE: You raised a ghost tonight.

JOAN *laughs*.

JOAN: Spooky, spooky.

CYGNA: Give it flesh, Mr Politician. Give it flesh.

ROSE, CYGNA *and* JOAN *disappear into the shadows*.

CYGNA: Call on us, when they betray you.

JOAN: We will on you.

BEATY: What are you –

ROSE: Delegates. Delegates, Comrade Minister.

They have gone. FEAST, *shouting after them:*

FEAST: You represent nothing!

BEATY (*low*): Or do they?

FEAST: Activisits crawl away from us, into holes.

BEATY (*low*): Holes, under walls.

FEAST: My daughter's got it. Terminal Maoism. Or 'Small is beautiful' anarchy – of some bloom. The boils look the same.

BEATY *tries a laugh*.

BEATY: Maybe they know something we don't.

FEAST: Come on Beaty. That mumbo-jumbo can't get to you. That's nothing to do with the grind of actually being a Socialist Government trying to run this bloody country. The scene on the far left is one big hospital for ideological disorders. Get to the car.

BEATY (*aside*): The Government car. Little curtains in the back window. Careering through the streets. Inside, a Minister, 'careering.' Frightened to look out. Did the streets speak to me with these women? What are people really thinking, what do they feel, what do they want? Is the Revolution won or lost, Jack Beaty?

FEAST: Jack!

BEATY (*aside*): Stop the car. Get out. Show my face?

Scene Four

A bathroom in 10 Downing Street. DUNN *and* MURGATROYD. DUNN *is in the bath.*

DUNN: Have we got the American Ambassador's body?

MURGATROYD: The head. The Special Branch are looking for the other bits.

DUNN: God I need a holiday. Or a good back rub. I 'phoned the President, half-an-hour ago.

MURGATROYD: To say what?

DUNN: Woops, sorry.

MURGATROYD: Was he pleased?

DUNN: Oh m'bones, m'dreaming bones. Have m' shoulder blades – slide out under the skin – and scraped. If I laid on 'floor, would you walk up my spine? – no forget that.

MURGATROYD: No going back.

DUNN: What?

MURGATROYD: Going back. After –

DUNN: Oh. In life, maybe not. But in politics – y'can always go back.

(*Low*:) Promised the President the body. Sneak it out of Heathrow. Old tea-chest or something.

MURGATROYD: The far left will go potty.

DUNN: I know I know! But I live in 'real world. Real life, y'know. Backache. National debt. Wear and tear. Inflation. Wondering why y'pee comes out bloody in the john, late some nights.

MURGATROYD: You want an international loan.

DUNN: If we were 'old-style bourgeois government – one 'phone call and I'd have had a Swedish masseuse in here, giving me a special.

MURGATROYD: A loan. From the IMF. From the Americans –

DUNN: Still. Party's anti-sexist stand kissed goodbye to all that.

MURGATROYD: We wink at the sacking of their Embassy, damn well nearly condone the assassination of their Ambassador –

DUNN: Negotiating position. If y'not got a position of strength –

DUNN *shrugs.*

MURGATROYD: Get one of terror –

DUNN (*angrily*): Two real worlds, actually. Soviets or them.

(*Wagging two fingers*:) Two! Sup wi' one or the other!

MURGATROYD: The KGB or Coca-Cola?

DUNN: Weakening, Henry?

DUNN *lifts a little cup of water and pours it over his upturned face.*

MUGRATROYD: We can't –

DUNN: You know I'd go for a treaty o' friendship with 'Soviet Union. But oh no. British democratic tradition. All right. She's got two tits, sweet Mother Earth – one East one West. We all find ourselves on one or –

He sighs.

The other. Ha! And I still get heckled as 'Paternalist', 'Stalinist pig.'

He splashes the water, angry again.

Thirty-seven years hard I've done. Street corner. More meetings than hot dinners. Union and Party, Branch, District, National Executive. And now I lead a Socialist Government. And do I, under the pressure, in between sandwiches, the 'phone calls, betray its very name?

DUNN *sags.*

MURGATROYD: Bill –

DUNN: I am so tired. So successful and so tired.

DUNN, *splashing again.*

The great sea of a Socialist Party! But am I riding 'waves or being smashed on 'beach? Cut me.

MURGATROYD: What?

DUNN *lifts a pumice stone out of the water.*

DUNN: From the shoulder blades down to the small of me back.

MURGATROYD: Oh all right.

MURGATROYD *takes the pumice stone. He stares at it.*

DUNN: Go on.

MURGATROYD: Right.

He runs the pumice stone from DUNN's *shoulder blades down to the small of his back.*

DUNN: They used to argue, where does 'soul live? Heart? Head? Testicles, vagina? No. In 'muscular wall of your back.

He grabs MURGATROYD's *hand.*

Late night colley-wobbles all this, in me bath. Not a word of it. Soviet Union, smashed on a beach. I go down, you go down.

MURGATROYD: And down goes sanity.

DUNN: What? Oh. Yes.

Ever since I got here, to Number Ten, I've had a bath at midnight. Bad habit. Know why?

MURGATROYD: No, Bill.

He hands DUNN *the pumice stone.*

DUNN: Before I became Prime Minister, every midnight, for three and a half decades, I'd go for a walk..Wherever I was. To look at the streets, listen. Now I do not dare.

He looks at the pumice stone then tosses it into the water.

Instead I wash myself.

BEATY, FEAST *and* ROSS *come on. They hesitate.*

DUNN: N' n' n' no, come in! To m' bathroom!

FEAST (*low*): We have.

BEATY (*low*): Sh.

DUNN: Well?

An embarrassed silence.

MURGRATROYD: Bill, you asked for an inner Cabinet, at midnight –

DUNN: I know that. Well, Jack?

BEATY: Well, Bill?

DUNN: I hear on the News you're an English hero. Bring me my bow of burning gold, eh?

He looks at them in turn.

Eh?

He smiles. They begin to smile.

After tonight, the Yanks go home at last, eh?

FEAST: A socialist Britain, free of the spheres of influence, Russia and America.

DUNN: Yes, thank you Sonny. Henry! Towel. Ross! Clothes. Suit for 8 a.m. briefing. Be up from now 'til then.

MURGATROYD *with a towel,* ROSS *goes off and comes back on with clothes and a suit on a hanger.* DUNN *gets out of the bath and wraps the towel around him like a toga, as he talks.*

Comrades! How many years hard? All our life-times. Years hard, for the Party to be built. Years hard to come to power. And now, years facing us to get any socialism into daily life at all.

He stumbles. The others glance at each other.

BEATY: All right, Bill?

DUNN *points at the suit.*

DUNN: Why isn't there a check handkerchief in that breast pocket? I said I wanted a check handkerchief in that breast pocket.

ROSS: There is, Bill.

Delicately ROSS *pulls a check handkerchief up out of the top pocket.*

DUNN: Right.

He hitches his towel.

There'll be a lot of hoo-ha. I want a show of solidarity. Jack here's invited us all up to his neck of the woods for 'weekend.

BEATY: Have I?

FEAST: You have now.

DUNN: Brass Band Gala. In your constituency. Asked me to speak and all, haven't you Lad.

BEATY: Why not –

DUNN: Don't mind me pulling your balls on this one do you, Jack?

BEATY: My balls are in your gift.

DUNN: Hunky dory.

MURGATROYD (*to* ROSS): Ah – a. He's wearing the accent extra thick. This means murder.

ROSS: What?

DUNN: So. Weekend off.

He ruffles BEATY's *hair.*

How d'you think this son of the bourgeoisie got his hands on 'working-class constituency – Brass Band Gala and all? Pass y'self off as some kind of red, did you Jack?

Eh?

False laughter.

MURGATROYD (*low*): Blood, blood.

Scene Five

JENNY GAZE, *reading a letter.*

GAZE: 'They talked of politics to end politics. The power of the streets. I felt a terrible, secret joy. My love, I heard your voice in what they said.'

She screws the letter up and throws it away.

Why must the good always be weak?

JACK BEATY *comes on.*

BEATY: Bill Dunn's coming up by train. In the morning. For the Gala.

A silence.

I drove up, to get here before the circus. You've been reading my letter.

Jenny?

He tries to embrace her. She turns away.

I haven't slept for two nights. I'm – wildly happy. But it's dangerous. Dangerous days! I think they're losing their grip, Jenny. They can't govern. I think it's even beginning to get to Bill Dunn. The old way, Cabinet deals, pushing back-benchers about, a favour in the Party there, a threat there – it's coming apart! There'll have to be a massive extension of democracy, right through the movement–

GAZE: Oh shut up!

A silence.

BEATY: What's the matter?

GAZE: You babble, you –

She turns away again.

Get back to your wife if it's pillow talk you want. About what a big boy you are, taking on the government.

BEATY: What-is-the-matter?

There is always something the matter when you bring up my wife.

GAZE: Come up to your Northern love nest. To step out of your clothes and be admired.

Go on, get back to her. Let her breathe warm air on your neck to puff you up.

BEATY: My love, I –

She hits him.

All right! All right!

All right.

GAZE: The matter, what's the matter? Everything we believe in. 'The matter' you talk of endlessly, smoking in bed. Weep for, lying on my tit. Night after night in adultery. 'The matter' of a socialist Britain.

BEATY: You don't realise. Unless I am very sharp, they'll lay the corpse of the American Ambassador at my feet. I'm pushing a corpse around –

GAZE: Then chop it up. Feed it to your kids.

BEATY: God. If this century's going to flower it had better get one green leaf up above the mud, quick.

GAZE: Ha!

BEATY: 'Ha' meaning?

GAZE: A political argument with you is like trying to have a conversation under water. What is the special relationship of Britain to America? Rape, I think. Unreported out of shame. My country is a woman in a dark park. America whispers 'Scream and it'll be worse.' And down she lays. And he stuffs the lot up her – from intercontinental missiles in East Anglian lanes to 'Hawaii Five-O' up her TV tubes. 'Thank you' whimpers Britannia, through clenched teeth.

The politics we have betray us. To America. To the greed of a vicious few at home. Betrays me, an Englishwoman. So don't ask me, Mr Politician, to step out of my clothes and love you. I am a victim of rape. Right now I'd rather masturbate with broken glass than have you.

BEATY: What – do you want me to do?

GAZE: Get – the – politics.

BEATY: Get the politics. Yes. Right. I'll nip out to a take-away.

A silence.

I can't find the politics.

GAZE: I can. Our so-called Marxist Prime Minister, who comes here by train tomorrow to hear the workers play brass bands – was on the 'phone to the President of the United States of America – while the smoke was still in the eagle's feathers.

He wants an American loan.

BEATY: Bill Dun.

GAZE: Bill Dunn.

BEATY: No.

GAZE: Think it.

BEATY: No.

GAZE: Think it then do it.

BEATY: How do you know that?

GAZE: I know.

A silence.

BEATY: If that were true, and I can't believe it's true – we'll vote him down.

GAZE: Ha.

BEATY: In the Party, in the Commons.

GAZE: And force a General Election? Would a Socialist Party win again, right now, in Britain?

BEATY: If we can't, we have no right to be the government.

GAZE: Socialists have every right to be the government.

BEATY: Majority vote or no?

GAZE: You believe in a vanguard in power or you don't. Political power is political power. Got by the farce of a General Election or other means.

BEATY: I see corpses when you talk like that. Strung on the wire of camps, stretching for miles. We can't betray an elected Socialist Government.

GAZE: It's betrayed itself. Its leader has lifted a telephone and sold us to America.

BEATY: So what do you suggest? Tomorrow in my home I take the Prime Minister into the toilet and knife him?

GAZE (*calls out*): Ross!

ROSS *comes on.*

BEATY: Ross.

ROSS: Jack.

BEATY: You've got a habit of walking out of dark corners.

ROSS: Good. Then let me give you a thought from a dark corner.

A silence.

Do you know how vast the security system of this country is? How deep it lies, in the landscape, in the streets, waiting? Telephone lines, TV and radio masts, the Cornish cliffs to the Norfolk Broads, to the Clyde to the Northern Isles – linking secret operations rooms in odd buildings in the suburbs, in market towns, on the top floors of office blocks in city centres? And do you know how many men and women, in the police, the Special Branch, the Army, the intelligence services, the Civil Defence, drill, week in week out, to work those rooms?

All this trouble is gone to in case one of two things happen. A nuclear war with the Soviet Union or civil disorder at home. 'Civil disorder at home' meaning 'A Revolution'.

The system is very professional. It aches, it drools, for orders to obey. It's a giant, sleeping just beneath our daily lives. Ready to take over courts, TV, press, Parliament, even the Cabinet.

Here is the dark thought.

What if a bunch of determined men and women – ?

A silence.

How many years have we known each other, Jack? Since we were kids, sitting on the roads to nuclear power stations. On the 'phone 'til three a.m. trying to screw up the right-wing in the local Labour Party? We were very young. Yet here we are. Tonight in this room. And with an opportunity. You, for the moment, able to jam the streets. I, no doubt for the moment, with responsibility for internal security. It couldn't be done without you. I am a policeman, but you're a leader. Look. It's there. Now. In front our faces.

He makes a grasping gesture before his face.

The means for the Dictatorship of the Proletariat.

He makes a little laugh.

Funny. Trotsky, Lenin, on the night of the 11th October, 1917, were just men in a room. And younger than us.

I'm next door.

He hestitates, then goes off.

GAZE: Yes, he and I are lovers. Yes, we talk about you. Yes, I slept with him long before I dragged you away from your long-suffering, and loving wife.

What do you expect? Sexual fidelity? I am a political animal and a woman in a man's world. I despise women who say 'I am a woman' and don't say, in the same breath, 'I am a revolutionary socialist.'

BEATY: An armed coup.

A silence. Then he shouts.

Ross!

Scene Six

DUNN, MURGATROYD, ROSS, FEAST *and* BEATY *come on. They carry pint mugs of beer, except for* ROSS *who carries a pint mug of orange juice. They wear plastic mackintoshes over their suits and are wet.*

DUNN: Umpa umpa, stick it up your jumper. Brass band music. Sound like the movement of healthy bowels. I love it. Pity about rain. Still!

(*He raises his glass:*) To Lads and Lassies with the puff!

The others mumble and sip.

MURGATROYD: Good speech, Bill.

DUNN: Meant every word. Backwards.

Laughter.

(*To* ROSS:) Can't you just have an half? Bloody carrot juice.

ROSS: Orange. Orange juice.

DUNN: Don't look right, Cabinet Minister walking off platform of Brass Band Gala with a pint of carrot juice in his hand. What do you lace it with, blood?

Laughter and glances.

Someone get him a pint!

MURGATROYD *slips away.*

Day's a day for getting tipsy on 'grass, muddy though it be. Good for us, a beano like this. Eh Bernard?

FEAST: It's a shock. Just to see people in their thousands, out of doors. A minister never goes on the tube, on a bus, in a pub. Your world is committee rooms, TV studios, the back seats of government cars. You end up never hearing how people talk.

DUNN: Aye. It's nice to be reminded 'working class is really there.

MURGATROYD *comes on with a pint of beer.*

Eh up! Here we go.

DUNN *takes the pint from* MURGATROYD.

There you are Ross.

MURGATROYD *and* FEAST *on the side.*

MURGATROYD: Funny how we never use Ross's first name.

FEAST: Maybe he sees himself as an idea, more than a man.

MURGATROYD: Indeed.

DUNN *and* ROSS *stare at each other. Then* ROSS *takes the pint of beer and* DUNN *takes the pint of orange juice from him.* DUNN *sloshes the orange juice offstage and throws the pint pot after it. He raises his glass.*

DUNN: Gentlemen. Prosperity, health and peace of every working man and woman on these islands. You'll drink to that, Ross.

DUNN *chinks his glass against* ROSS's. *They all look at* ROSS. *Then he sips.* DUNN *roars and slaps* ROSS *on the back. Beer splashes.*

Give me men who're half cut. Decision making may be a bit unpredictable but it'll be human.

He puts his arm round BEATY. *They keep their public smiles speaking privately.*

Your feelings comradely to me, Jack?

BEATY: I'd never – split the Party.

DUNN: Personally. Personally. I've been a father to you. No don't pull away, y'pull away. Don't like people much, do you?

BEATY: I –

DUNN: They'll never live what you want, y'see Jack. People. Bits fall of 'em, they wander away – can't live it all the time, y'see. Human perfection. That being what you're after, eh?

BEATY (*hesitates*): Yes.

DUNN (*very low*): You're riding high, Jack. But I'm going to screw you.

I want you to know.

He squeezes BEATY *and goes public again.*

And now with our hero to the Grand Hotel. Then to a little party of my own. To which you will all bloody well come. Drink yourselves silly. Forget politics for a night. Talk about gardening, love, football. Y'know – real life!

Scene Seven

A bedroom in the Grand Hotel. BEATY *alone.*

BEATY: 'Once and for all.' 'A decisive blow.' 'The dash for Socialism.' All the slogans coming home to roost. Black crows on the chimneys of the Grand Hotel, in a northern English town.

Do it now. After all the agendas, party conferences – it comes down to this. Boot in a hotel door at night. Kill a drunken man. Simple. Brutal. The politics is in the consequences.

And consequences of consequences. I can't think. There's a little theatre in my head. Right and wrong shout at each other like actors.

GAZE *comes on.*

What's happening?

GAZE: They're still drinking. Why aren't you in there?

BEATY: Did he ask for me?

GAZE: Of course.

BEATY: We can't do this.

GAZE: You mean it won't work.

BEATY: Morally.

GAZE: Why does it slip away from you again and again? One moment you're a grown man with experience, the next you're a child. Or idiot – vacant eyes, amnesia. Why do you always go back to nothing? Why do you have to convince yourself, over and over from scratch, every second?

BEATY: Endorse political murder, for crying out aloud – in England.

GAZE: Oh I'll cry out loud. Why do the English call themselves 'moral'? The rest of the world knows we're a race of ruthless bastards who stamped all over a quarter of the planet. Tore nations apart. Distorted continents.

And now our Empire's gone, we're not left standing in the pure air of a high, moral plateau. We're one more nasty little European country, trying to get our politics up out of the slime.

BEATY: Just – be quiet.

Let me think. Let me feel.

GAZE: I tell you, my love, if tonight all you want to do is 'think' and 'feel' – you had better slink away from this hotel. Go and dig your garden.

BEATY: All right!

All right.

But, you see, I have a thought in my head. It grows. It pushes against my skull. It pressures every other thought. It has got to the nerves of my eyes. So I see, even in the world outside, the strands of the thought, looping every movement of my fellow human beings, tangling, pulling everything, by a terrible logic into one hard knot.

He laughs.

The presumption. I fear the English Revolution is a tumour in my brain.

My mind.

GAZE: I've had the thought for years.

She laughs.

If it's a disease it's in my blood. Political VD? I don't think they treat that on the NHS. And you and I are dripping with it, along with hundreds of thousands.

BEATY: I hope here are hundreds of thousands.

GAZE: Millions. Many not yet born.

BEATY: If we're wrong –

GAZE: Then I'll cut out my own sex.

BEATY *scoffs.*

Don't you believe me?

BEATY: Oh I do. 'My love.'

GAZE: Then.

BEATY: Then.

A silence.

GAZE: Ha!

BEATY: What?

GAZE: 'A sexual thought.'

BEATY: Yes.

GAZE: Both of us naked, touching with our tongues.

BEATY: Yes.

Scene Eight

A gentlemen's lavatory in the Grand Hotel. BEATY, his face wet, as if before a wash-basin and mirror. He has a paper towel. He pulls the skin around his eyes. FEAST comes on, as if out of a cubicle, straightening his clothes. He struggles against drink and fatigue.

FEAST: The sins of the fathers. I feel terrible. Oh.

He goes off. A lavatory flushes. He comes back on.

Funny how when you come up north your stool changes.

He focuses on BEATY.

Jack?

BEATY *still stares in the mirror.*

Jack Beaty?

BEATY *whirls round and stares at* FEAST.

You OK?

BEATY: What's the time?

FEAST: Ah.

He consults a digital watch.

Digitally. Three. Thirteen. A.M. Why do they give tenths of seconds? Who can tell a tenth of a second? These things chop time up. Little bombs. Blip blip.

BEATY: Is Bill Dunn –

FEAST: The Prime Minister is drunkenly asleep. Between two chairs. There is a smell of urine and happiness.

BEATY: Why are you –

FEAST: Hotel's got to me. Corridors. Pipes. We in the middle of a ship? There a night sky up there? Moon? What's that bit in Orwell? The torturer says the sky's just twenty feet above the building. And the stars are light bulbs lit by the Ministry of Truth.

BEATY: Go to bed.

FEAST: Right.

FEAST goes to turn then stops.

Those women.

BEATY: What about them?

FEAST: Do you think about what they said?

BEATY: No.

FEAST: Your face on placards, above mass demonstrations?

BEATY: No.

A silence.

FEAST: Liar.

BEATY: Goodnight Bernard.

FEAST (*slurring*): Don't unleash deep-lying social forces. Let deep-lying social forces –

He hiccups.

Lie. Hiccups now. Night night.

FEAST goes off. BEATY, staring at his face.

BEATY: Your dead stand behind you Jack Beaty. In a lavatory mirror.

Our age began. They divided up the fields. The peasants lost their rights. The human spirit invented Manchester. Or something invented Manchester. The families drifted from the land. The working class found itself born, into a cramped, filthy room. The ceiling as low as a coal-face. The walls screeching with cotton machines. The floor the street of a slum with an open drain. The industrial revolution. A concentration camp in slow motion, decades long. And for basic dignity, against the cruelty of history and the sufferings of daily life – the inmates of the nineteenth century invented Socialism.

Gave you what literacy you have, Jack Beaty. What health. What sense of justice. Right and wrong.

He looks over his shoulder.

Judge, comrades. If I am wrong tonight come out of your graves. Tear my mind to pieces.

Scene Nine

A corridor in the Grand Hotel. A telephone rings throughout the scene. JENNY GAZE alone.

GAZE: It's there. A fire. How many floors away? Up or down? A tang in the air, cutting, like acid. They're doing it! Doors kicked in. Drunks and public men choking in the smoke.

She sniffs.

Don't know – that 'phone! Oh is it being done or not?

BEATY (*off*): Bitch! Bitch!

GAZE: The years of talk. We've got the arguments but where is the will?

BEATY runs on, banging against the walls of the corridor. He is soaking wet. He holds a handkerchief against his mouth with one hand, with the other he clutches something beneath his coat. He leans against the wall.

You're soaked –

BEATY: Sprinkler system. Want me burning, bitch? A human torch eh?

BEATY fighting for his breath. GAZE shouts.

GAZE: What happened? Is Bill Dunn alive?

BEATY: Oh he's alive. With his head half off. He's alive, with his corpse burning.

GAZE: What –

BEATY: His Special Branch bodyguard – wouldn't move! All Ross's creatures. They were ready for the fire, with masks. But they stood and stared. At me! For me to do it!

GAZE: So –

BEATY: So! Smashed the little glass cupboard in the corridor, didn't I. Went in and cut him to bits, didn't I. See?

He opens his coat. He holds an axe. His shirt, arm and hands are covered with blood. He laughs.

Up to now I thought the deadliest political weapon was the telephone.

GAZE: The bodyguards –

BEATY: Promote them! Promote them all!

Three brand new Colonels in the brand new Secret Police. We're going to need a brand new Secret Police, aren't we, bitch?

GAZE: For Godsake –

BEATY: Don't worry, bitch. I got to the end of the corridor – and closed the firedoors on them.

They stare at each other. A silence but for the telephone ringing.

GAZE: And the fire alarms –

BEATY: Little stickler in't you.

Ross cut into the circuits. They'll go off when the fire gets hold. Good and true.

GAZE: So.

BEATY: So.

GAZE: The Grand Hotel of government –

BEATY: Is burning down. Good and true.

He begins to weep.

GAZE: Stop that!

BEATY: No –

GAZE: Come here –

BETY: No –

GAZE: Get all this off –

GAZE, pulling at his clothes.

BEATY: A shower before the thirteenth floor caves in?

GAZE: Quickly.

BEATY grips her.

BEATY: Come in under with me. Let the tap melt hot metal on us, the water boil us alive.

GAZE, gripping him.

GAZE: Listen to me! In the morning people will pick through the ruins. And we'll walk among them, modestly, with serious faces, inwardly screaming with joy.

Fire alarm bells go off. They are gripping each other. A blackout.

Scene Ten

*The smouldering ruins of the Grand Hotel.
Dawn. Rain. FEAST and
MURGATROYD close together, at a
distance from ROSS. ROSS with a small,
black two-way radio set which he holds
close to his mouth.*

*FEAST has an umbrella, his clothes are
torn. MURGATROYD is in his pyjamas,
with a coat over them.*

MURGATROYD: I can't stop shivering.

FEAST: What are we walking about in the
ruins for? I've been walking about in the
ruins for an hour.

MURGATROYD: What?

FEAST: We feel it should be done. Cabinet
Minister. Be seen. Give interviews. Go
through the cordon – walk in the ruins.

I think I'm still drunk.

MURGATROYD: I 'phoned my wife. She
burst into tears when I told her. I stared at
the ear bit. And thought – oh yes, we
loved Bill Dunn, and he's dead. I'm in my
'jamas.

*ROSS's radio crackles, the words
inaudible. He whispers into it.*

*FEAST glances at ROSS then back to
MURGATROYD.*

FEAST: What?

MURGATROYD: Why I'm shivering. Oh
my God, what are we going to do? I loved
him too. Brutal bugger, but real, heavy
with it.

FEAST: 'Years hard.'

MURGATROYD: 'Years hard.'

FEAST: As he said, a hundred times a day.

MURGATROYD: I was close to him, I've
got to step into his clothes. And I'm in my
'jamas –

FEAST: Henry, have you seen your Private
Secretary this morning?

MURGATROYD: Fly sod's round here
somewhere.

FEAST: Mine went from the Hotel before
midnight.

A silence.

Without telling me.

MURGATROYD: Before –

FEAST: Before the fire.

A silence.

MURGATROYD: Ha! What are you
saying? Rats – a ship?

FEAST: I hope I am still drunk.

*GAZE comes on. She draws ROSS aside
and whispers to him. He nods.*

MURGATROYD: What's that cow doing
here? Inside the cordon –

*GAZE glances at MURGATROYD and
FEAST goes off.*

Evil-minded whore.

FEAST: Shut up. We've all known for years
that woman is Jack Beaty's political wife –

MURGATROYD: 'Political wife!' Funny
name for it –

FEAST: Oh come on. And how is
Sally-Ann?

MURGATROYD: Oh –

FEAST: Yes 'Oh.'

ROSS, the radio.

MURGATROYD: He's talking into his
walky-talky again.

FEAST: You've noticed that.

MURGATROYD: I've been worried
politically before. Worried sick. My
ulcers are the scars to prove it. But I've
never felt – political fear.

We'll drive. Now. Heathrow in four
hours. A 'plane to the States.

FEAST: No. No – wait for the inner cabinet
meeting.

MURGATROYD: Have you been called
to an inner cabinet meeting?

FEAST: In the hour –

MURGATROYD: Have you?

A silence.

Have you been called to a cabinet
meeting?

FEAST: No.

They stare at each other. A silence.

Suddenly I feel we've got to talk to each
other, fast – the next time we see each

other may be in a cell –

FEAST: You're having a nightmare, Henry. Wake up.

MURGATROYD: I've always known one rainy dawn I'd not wake up and live on in – the nightmare. Of it all going wrong.

(*He scoffs*:) When you've had a job at the heart of government, in the actual pumping, blood and muscle centre – you know how weak it is. How thin the walls –

FEAST: We've only ourselves to blame.

I think there could be –

He hesitates.

An Emergency Government.

MURGATROYD: 'Emergency Government', that the phrase? Coronary of the body politic, eh?

He tries to laugh.

FEAST: That's what the neglect of democracy leads to, has been leading to for years.

MURGATROYD: And who will lead this 'Emergency Government?' That policeman over there?

He gestures at ROSS, *who sees him do so and turns a full circle away, his mouth at the radio.*

That woman? Not Jack Beaty. He'd have nothing to do with it. I mean –

(*He tries to scoff:*) What are we talking about? An armed coup?

FEAST: We think Civil Liberty is as natural as a cow. Standing in a field, glimpsed from a train window. Always there, solid in the rain, chewing the cud. But easily, oh easily, the next time the public takes a train – they could look out and see the field concreted over, blood-stained, the poor beast hacked to bits.

MURGATROYD: What do you know – what do you think you know – Bernard – ?

FEAST: For my sins, I'm close to Jack Beaty. Do you get the impression, Henry, you and I have been allowed, just for a while, to talk together like this?

MURGATROYD: We must – must –

FEAST: What?

MURGATROYD: Save the country.

FEAST: Ha!

MURGATROYD: Appeal? –

FEAST: To whom?

MURGATROYD: The people?

FEAST: How?

MURGATROYD: TV –

FEAST: Do you think you and I will ever get near a television studio again?

And anyway, old friend, what – would – you say? Sorry?

A silence.

MURGATROYD: Sorry.

MURGATROYD *screws his eyes tight and lowers his head.*

FEAST: Sorry you were a young man who believed in Socialism. And forgot it when you were older.

Sorry you were a minister in a Socialist government – and became a hatchet man.

Sorry you nailed up lips with threats or promises. Silenced Party Branches.

Sorry your skull grew thick. Your mind blocked. The hard head of a hard man, behind the political throne of a hard man.

MURGATROYD (*low*): All right. All right, you bastard.

FEAST (*low*): Walk away now. Through the police cordon if you can. It's a four hour drive to Heathrow. I'll put in a word to get you away.

Go on! Maybe they've not got things tight yet.

MURGATROYD: Comrade –

FEAST: Please. I – don't want your blood on my hands.

MURGATROYD: God what a thing to say.

ROSS *comes towards them suddenly.*

FEAST: Too late.

ROSS: Gentlemen, you are under arrest.

Scene Eleven

A summer garden. BEATY *and* FEAST.

BEATY: Bernard. It's so good to see you. Come out into the garden.

They walk forward, BEATY *holding* FEAST*'s arm.*

FEAST: God.

BEATY: Yes, hollyhocks. Didn't know I gardened, did you?

He giggles.

A Suffolk country garden. See that mulberry tree? A present from the General Council of the TUC.

FEAST: It's –

BEATY: A small tree, yes. A long time growing. When it's grown to maturity we'll all be dead. But what do you expect from the TUC?

Do you mind if I weed?

FEAST: No. No –

BEATY: Ross!

ROSS *glides on.*

A garden trowel.

ROSS *glides off.*

He sleeps with Jenny. You knew?

FEAST: No. No –

BEATY: Ah! You never had intelligence. I mean information. Intelligence of clear thought – that you had.

Still have, no?

FEAST: I've been in prison.

BEATY: Yes. I put you there.

(*He shouts:*) Ross! I called for a garden trowel! To dig up weeds! On the bloody lawn!

(*Touching* FEAST*'s arm:*) Don't worry, he'll come with one. Any moment now. Just wait.

FEAST: Jack –

BEATY: Sh.

ROSS *comes on with a brand new garden trowel in a cellophane wrapping. He holds it out to* BEATY.

Gloves, man.

ROSS *takes a pair of kitchen gloves, also brand new, from his pocket.* BEATY *takes the gloves and trowel from* ROSS. *He hands the trowel to* FEAST, *who stares at it.*

No, I'll break the wrapping.

BEATY *stares at* ROSS.

Thank you Ross. Now go away.

ROSS *turns away, stops, then glides off.* BEATY, *breaking the sealed kitchen gloves and putting them on.*

You know, of course, this country cottage is not what it seems. It is the entrance to a Regional Seat of Government. I move from one to the other of these underground bunkers, with their entrances disguised by English cottage gardens. Did they beat you up?

FEAST: In Brixton Gaol? No.

BEATY: Kitchen gloves. The English countryside is safe compared to others. One poisonous snake. Owls, which can come at your face at night. Wasps, nettles. But nothing that kills. Except for the soil.

FEAST: ?

BEATY: Tetanus.

FEAST: Yes?

BEATY: Lockjaw. What disease can be more fatal for a politician, eh?

He giggles.

Eh?

He nudges FEAST *with his elbow.*

Bernard?

FEAST: What do you want?

A silence.

BEATY: Trowel.

FEAST *throws the trowel away.*

FEAST: I was brought here in a police van. On the way, my bowels opened. Thought I was, at long last, being taken to my death you see.

They're going to do it to me outside London, I thought, looking through the little window.

By the sea, or on a cliff. Or in the countryside, shot in a quarry?

But I was given a bath and these clothes. And pushed into this garden with you. To watch you put on rubber gloves – and weed a lawn.

A silence.

BEATY: Oliver Cromwell was a farmer. Lose yourself in nature? The price of cereals. The annual fix of the Milk Marketing Board. I feel the sense of it, going to kneel on this lawn to dig out dandelions. Over the underground tunnels of RSG number 22. Peace in work.

Looking at his gloved hands.

Henry Murgatroyd is in California.

A silence.

Did you hear from him?

FEAST: In Brixton?

BEATY: You have privileges.

FEAST: A telephone in my cell? A telex? Let alone unopened mail, or visits from my family –

BEATY: You know what I mean.

FEAST: You bastard.

BEATY: You do me an injustice.

FEAST: I do you –

BEATY: Yes. I invite you to my country home –

FEAST: You had me brought here in a black maria! And this is no home. It's a fort. For all the hollyhocks –

BEATY: I think you are under a delusion, Bernard.

FEAST: And what delusion is that, Jack?

BEATY: That you are not free.

FEAST: Oh.

BEATY: The day after the fire – why did you help Murgatroyd get on a plane to America? Bribe an official – spend the last shred of your influence, to free him? And not yourself?

Nothing from FEAST.

Are you in touch with him?

FEAST: I told you, I am in prison –

BEATY: Do –

Do –

You believe there is a class war going on in our country?

FEAST: Yes of course. What do you want, a catechism? I'm still a Socialist –

BEATY: How do you think this class war will –

A flowing gesture with his rubber covered hands.

Turn out?

FEAST: I hope for the victory of the working class.

BEATY: Mmm.

FEAST: How 'Mmm?'

BEATY: Mmmm, by what means?

See, people demonstrate their support for my government. Every weekend. Streams of banners. TV. Gymnastic displays at Earls Court. Don't you see TV in Brixton? Category 'A' criminal like you?

They've even taken to putting flowers on the spot in that car-park, where you and I met those three women. Carnations.

FEAST: Funeral flower, isn't it, the carnation?

BEATY: No, just expensive. I want you to understand. I want to take you in my arms and love you as a brother.

FEAST: Ross's policemen put flowers in that car-park, every morning. No-one else. Admit it. Your regime's a mockery. Oh parliament still meets, the TV news still comes on, but it's all sham. Mockery. You've subverted everything, admit it, admit it.

BEATY: Yes. We're primitive. Primitive men and women.

He looks at his hands.

Our cruelty. Our personal spite. Our self-loathing. No wonder cripples come to power. Look! My hands are like claws.

FEAST: Christ! You really think you are Oliver Cromwell! One more reluctant axe-man.

BEATY (*low*): What do you mean?

FEAST: All the country knows you killed Bill Dunn with a fire-axe, from a glass panel in a corridor of the Grand Hotel.

Well, the whole of Brixton Gaol knows. As the saying goes, if you want to know the truth about a country, go to its prisons.

Terror bleeds truth, even through prison walls.

BEATY: With every word you say, you become more dangerous. You know that?

FEAST: Ex-politicians become philosophers, confined to their cells. We think a lot about justice.

He laughs.

And come to rule a country, justly. A country three-and-a-half metres long by two and a half metres wide, between a lavatory pan and a steel door with an eye in it.

Closing his eyes and shaking his head.

Tell me – bringing me here to your garden, what do you want? To torment me?

BEATY: It's all right Bernard –

He puts his arm round him.

Don't worry, don't –

A gesture with his hand.

You made a mistake. 'Murky Murgy' we used to call him in Bill Dunn's time, remember?

He raises a storm in America against everything you and I believe in.

He wants America to send troops. Troops, eh? Landing craft Penzance to Bognor Regis?

Ha! Now the man swims in his element. The 'Free Society' of America. Where pigs can grow fat, snort and churn in the mud. Murky Murgy has become an entrepreneur with a cause – himself. Where did you put my trowel?

FEAST *gestures vaguely.* BEATY, *ripping off the gloves.*

Christ! I'll never make a gardener. An Oliver Cromwell either, eh?

He throws the gloves off.

It's still me, Bernard. It's still Jack Beaty.

FEAST: What do you want from me? Comfort?

BEATY: Work. In my government. As Foreign Secretary. Against Murky Murgy. Against America. To join with the Third World. And at home – to be an honest voice, speaking clearly.

There, you old lag. How does that grab you?

FEAST *weeps.*

FEAST: You want me, just – simply – simply to kill myself –

BEATY: Comrade.

A Revolutionary Government has taken power. Good, I say. It has withdrawn British Troops from Northern Ireland. Good, I say, with all my heart. Cut off links with America. Good, I say. Not become a satellite of Russia. Good. Is working to make a nuclear-free zone in Europe. Do you, as a socialist, disagree with any of that?

FEAST: No.

BEATY: Then – what is your trouble?

FEAST: Prison.

He giggles.

Prison is my trouble.

BEATY: We have legislation in preparation for the worker's control of industry –

FEAST: Ha!

BEATY: Sorry?

FEAST: Sorry to you. What tyranny will ever legislate a democratic institution into being?

He laughs.

Worker's control!

Watch it Jack, they may vote the Tories back. And American missiles and three million unemployed. And vote you and your mistress and her policeman to hell.

BEATY (*low*): They would be stupid if they did.

FEAST: Oh agreed. Agreed! Agreed! Agreed! Agreed!

A silence.

BEATY: If you understand so much, why

did you help that pig Murgatroyd? You know he is an enemy of everything you believe in. Say 'Workers' Control' to his face and his eye would haemorrhoid.

FEAST: It was just –

He sighs.

Humanity.

BEATY: Ah.

FEAST: I –

BEATY: Ah.

FEAST: He is a pig of a man. In a just world – of no consequence.

And we must act as if the world is just. Else, how can we go on?

Yes, I engineered his escape.

And I stayed saying, yes. I'll serve my country's government. If I am not put in prison.

BEATY: It's wonderful to talk to a good man. Even though I have so greatly – abused him.

Go for a walk.

FEAST: How do you mean?

BEATY: Suffolk. A sunny day. The small fields, like an old fashioned mattress on a bed, eh? Go to the kitchen. Get a bottle of Chianti, cold, it's my favourite. And go and sit under a hedge, drink wine, think.

Then come back at nightfall. Have supper with Jenny and me. Tell us if you're going to be your country's Foreign Secretary.

FEAST: I'm not in gaol anymore? Just like that?

BEATY: Just like that.

FEAST's legs collapse beneath him. He weeps. BEATY cradles him.

FEAST: I can't kill –

BEATY: No, no –

FEAST: Anyone, you see.

BEATY: No, comrade.

FEAST: Human.

BEATY: There there –

FEAST: Not send to their death, at the hands of the police –

BEATY: No –

FEAST: Not anyone.

BEATY: No, no comrade.

FEAST composes himself. He looks up at BEATY.

It's not manly, is it. To confess. Nor is it manly to be the confessor.

Oh – go into a field and get pissed.

FEAST: All right.

FEAST stands.

BEATY: The good are always weak, are they not?

FEAST: Yes, but we must persist.

BEATY: Indeed?

So – off you go.

FEAST: Yes.

BEATY (*aside*): He thinks he is a good man. Oh help him. Help me.

FEAST: I love you.

BEATY: Ha!

Be back, round seven-thirty, eight.

FEAST walks off. For the first time we see he has a limp. BEATY, after him.

We'll eat eh? Roast lamb, baby lamb!

(*Aside:*) Food, talk, in the evening of an English summer day. The fruit of privilege on our plate. Ha! I cut for the guest.

A slow gesture of a knife falling.

The meat dead and still. Yet so fresh and well-cooked, to the eater it almost lives.

(*He shouts:*) Ross!

(*Aside:*) I'd like to eat ideas. Chew arguments. Swallow conclusions. Pick my teeth free of little bits of information.

(*He shouts:*) Ross!

(*Aside:*) And wash it down – cold, thick, Sicilian wine of a decision made. Cutting the throat. Making the head – hot.

ROSS *wanders on.*

Take the surveillance team away from him.

ROSS *is about to speak.*

Send two men from the Special Unit. Heavies! Let them catch him by the side of a field. Behind a hedge. Let them bury him, up in the little wood. Reward them – cash from the 'B' fund.

And let them have accidents a few months from now.

Nothing from ROSS, *who turns to go.*

(BEATY *shouts*:) And tell the cook! Tonight, distilled water in the decanters!

ROSS *looks at him then turns and goes off.*

Tonight I'll toast you, Bernard. A glass of pure ideas, raised to the death of a good man.

He giggles. JENNY GAZE *comes on.*

GAZE: I saw Bernard Feast, go by the study window with a bottle of wine in his hand.

BEATY: And how do you think the bastard looked?

GAZE: He limped.

BEATY: Huh. What do you do with a good man who limps? Cut off his leg. Oh, then his body's no good. What do you do with that? Cut that off. Then there's just his memory. Words, he said. So, cut off any tongues that speak them? And bury the lot? Limbs? Torsos? Tongues? Yes! In a little wood, in the countryside! But then the trees will know. In their sap. In their leaves in the spring. Molecules of it, in their fibre. In the juice of it, in the hazels, in the acorns. Then burn the woods, eh? Napalm – bam! Concrete over the little hills. But – the ash. The dust from the fires. In the air! Oh! Into people's lungs. So they breathe – breathe – the words.

Oh Jenny. We could become the thing we seek to destroy.

GAZE: Stop it. Don't be alone. Keep close, among people –

BEATY: Every thought goes on and on – a bullet that richochets! Bam! Bam! Bam! On and on, 'til one simple thought means the whole world.

Ha! You look at a weed on a lawn and the jungles of Brazil rise up, growing into your eyes –

GAZE: Stop whirling. Stop. Get something to sleep.

BEATY: You're right. From now on I'll work at night, sleep in the day. A meal at eleven, midnight – start. And come the dawn, let the messages go out. The world of government gone dark to light, light to dark – the Civil Service with their minds torn to bits, eh?

Tea, now?

GAZE: My love, why do we have to think of ourselves as strong? All that matters is what is done.

BEATY *withdraws from her. A silence.*

BEATY: Tea.

Scene Twelve

BERNARD FEAST *alone, with a bottle of wine. He swigs. He sits down, the bottle between his legs. He massages his bad leg.*

FEAST: Two hopes. Two – hopes.

That men and women are not born evil. That's one.

He takes a swig from the bottle. He controls his breathing.

That there is the iron force of reason. With – which – we can make our history. That's s'other.

Mmm.

He pats the top of the bottle with the palm of his hand.

Two hopes. No Socialism without 'em.

We are good. Reason – is strong. Oh help us, help us. Who? To say 'Help' to? God the Father?

He stops patting the bottle. He snorts.

Is it the lot of persecuted revolutionaries, to end up believing in God? Like alcoholics on the wagon? Go away God! Get back down under the hedgerows, with the fungus.

He snorts.

God. And Gods. And magic. Mushroom faiths. We've only ourselves to say 'Help' to. Only us.

He pats the top of the bottle, slows then stops. Two bulky figures in black gear, their faces masked by helmets, approach him. They both carry automatic pistols with silencers. They stand before him. He looks up at them.

Comrades. A beautiful evening. The children will be in bed soon, all – across Britain.

A silence.

A dampness on the ground. Didn't notice, been drinking. But let it come down, eh? Water, steel or fire. I'll be safe in a ditch.

A silence.

Well?

What are you, religious, want my blessing?

He snorts.

You don't have it.

1ST MURDERER: No. We just enjoy our work.

FEAST: No.

Just – do it.

Don't – bits of me – or –

He flails with his heels to stand up.

Be humane.

Don't.

Look.

The 2ND MURDERER *laughs.* FEAST *stops flailing. He stares one to the other. They advance on him. They put the muzzles of their guns on his kneecaps and other parts of his body.*

1ST MURDERER: Now comrade, be reasonable.

The 1ST MURDERER *puts his gun at* FEAST's *neck.*

FEAST: Evil. Evil. Oh, what evil.

Scene Thirteen

The cottage's dining-room. A table set for dinner. Candelebra, glass, silver glittering. ROSS *and* BEATY.

ROSS: Like a rabbit.

BEATY: Yes.

ROSS: They said. Transfixed.

BEATY: Yes.

ROSS: They destroyed the face. Tore out the teeth. Cut off the finger prints. Burnt the body.

BEATY: Yes yes –

ROSS: You wanted a full report.

BEATY: What were his last words?

   ROSS *shrugs.*

   A full report!

ROSS: 'Oh what evil.'

   A silence.

BEATY: No that's not right –

ROSS: The report –

BEATY: No. Bernard Feast didn't believe in evil. That's not right.

ROSS: I assure you, Beaty –

BEATY: He did not say that! I knew Bernard Feast. He did not believe in evil!

   He paces. He turns on ROSS.

   And I'm not making some schoolboy debating point! Bernard had rationality in his bones.

   He wavers.

   No, that is not a full report.

ROSS: The bastard's dead. The body unidentifiable.

BEATY: But what got away?

ROSS: What could?

BEATY: Put a guard over the grave.

ROSS: Why?

BEATY: See what comes out of it!

ROSS: What?

   BEATY *pushes him in the chest and walks by him.*

BEATY: They will look like animals. Tiny, furry, white mice. But very tiny, tiny, tiny, as almonds.

Slipping away. In the leaves. Out of the wood. Down the hill. Onto the road. To the sea. Along the dunes. In holes along river banks. And into towns. In walls. Cellars. Plastered up chimneys. In rotting wood in the roofs.

And breeding. Little nests of chewed up paper!

They stare at each other.

His words.

ROSS: I'll burn the hillside. Will that make you happier?

BEATY: No no. No no.

He smiles and puts a hand on ROSS's *shoulder.*

ROSS: The Ambassador from Chad will be here any moment. His car passed the perimeter five minutes ago.

BEATY: Good good.

ROSS: I'll welcome him? Or you –

BEATY: No you.

   ROSS *hesitates.*

   Good.

ROSS *goes off, passing* JENNY GAZE *as she comes on. She wears evening dress.*

GAZE: Go out and meet the Ambassador.

BEATY: Let him come to me. Tonight I'll be the Pope.

GAZE: You neglect things. You sulk.

This man tonight is an Ambassador from the Third World. From a country that has had its revolutionary war. Wake up! We need all the friends we can get.

BEATY: Don't worry. I am briefed. Who is on the side of history, who is not – ha!

BEATY *turns away.* ROSS *comes on with the* AMBASSADOR, *who wears a Mao-like uniform. He is played by the* FEAST *actor, looking exactly like* FEAST.

AMBASSADOR: The Russians put States they help with aid into three categories. We have achieved category 'B'.

ROSS: Which is?

AMBASSADOR: How shall I put it? Railway rolling stock from the nineteen-fifties, but a first class cossack dancing company.

ROSS *and* GAZE *laugh politely. They all look at* BEATY, *whose back is still turned.*

ROSS: Ambassador, the Prime Minister.

The AMBASSADOR *holds out a hand.*

AMBASSADOR: Comrade –

BEATY *turns. A silence.*

GAZE: Jack?

A silence.

BEATY: Who did this?

AMBASSADOR: I am delighted to meet you.

BEATY: Who?

ROSS: Beaty what's the matter?

BEATY *crouches.*

ROSS: Beaty, what's the matter?

AMBASSADOR: Is –

ROSS: The Prime Minister is unwell.

AMBASSADOR (*smiling*): I am sorry to hear it. Leadership demands a heavy price, in human terms. Perhaps statesmanship is a wholly unnatural condition?

BEATY, *backing away.*

BEATY: Un –

AMBASSADOR: I have negotiated in the Kremlin! Believe me I know, in the midst of life we are in death –

He looks from one to the other, smiling.

BEATY (*low, to* GAZE): He's not black.

GAZE: You indulge yourself.

BEATY: He's not, he's not.

AMBASSADOR: ?

GAZE (*to the* AMBASSADOR): Mr Beaty has had fits from childhood. They pass. He insists his official programme is arranged and kept to the letter.

Perhaps we should go out on the lawn? It's a fine night –

BEATY: Tear his face off! Tear it off or I'll tear off mine –

AMBASSADOR (*to* ROSS): Perhaps a ruler. Between his teeth.

BEATY: Oh! A pun, old chum. Ruler – of a nation – me – in my own mouth? You want me to swallow myself?

A silence.

AMBASSADOR (*to* ROSS): I meant St Paul, too, was an epileptic.

ROSS: Yes, of course –

AMBASSADOR: Indeed, to us in the Third World, the victims of Christian missionaries over the centuries, the Pauline faith appears as an ideology conceived in a hallucinatory fit.

ROSS: Yes?

BEATTY: So why aren't you black? Why do you stand there with a white face?

A silence.

Well?

ROSS (*gutterally to* BEATY): For godsake, the man's a black African.

BEATY: Then who plastered a white mask on him! (*To the* AMBASSADOR:) Please, understand. You are either a trick. A ghost. Or madness –

AMBASSADOR (*angrily*): None of those things, Comrade Prime Minister.

I am simply a man from a poor country few have heard of and none care for. I had thought Britain had come to see herself in a similar light. Desperate light? A lonely little island, in a dark and dangerous continent?

BEATY: Whatever you are, I want to kill you.

AMBASSADOR: Huh! Africa has had many of you. Sane madmen. Huh! Now sick Europe is in for its quota.

He points at ROSS.

You!

I want safe guarantees for me and my embassy staff, back to Chad.

ROSS: Of course –

AMBASSADOR: The withdrawal will be complete in forty-eight hours.

ROSS: Yes.

AMBASSADOR (*to* BEATY): Prime Minister.

BEATY: Bernard?

ROSS *and* GAZE *stare at each other.*

AMBASSADOR: What was it your poet William Blake, meant by the saying – 'The cut worm forgives the plough'?

BEATY: Depends. Are you the worm, am I the plough? Or are you the plough and I – the worm.

AMBASSADOR: You, ask me?

BEATY (*chanting*): Get him out get him out get him out –

ROSS: One diplomatic channel –

AMBASSADOR: The Cuban Embassy.

ROSS: Telex?

BEATY: Out! Out! Out! Out!

GAZE *and the* AMBASSADOR *going off.*

ROSS: I will telephone ahead for a motorcycle escort.

AMBASSADOR: Appreciated.

They've gone.

BEATY (*aside*): Nothing wrong.

Actually, if people around me would only concentrate they would see that things, really, are very well.

I am so desperate. Lines go out of my hands for miles, into factories, streets, kitchens, bedrooms. Well – into police stations.

I flap my hands! Make my hands light! Feathers! Light, of no consequence, who doesn't smile at a bird, fluttering, over water, brilliant, blazing, in a moment of no – meaning, power –

No.

Suddenly I understood why dictators have themselves carved in stone, in every corner of a country. Utterly fixed.

He clamps his hands on his knees.

It's because they're terrified to move their hands.

GAZE *and* ROSS *come on.*

ROSS: If you dare to think you're indispensable, if you dare to think that –

BEATY: The history of revolutions is that secret policemen come and go, but what has to be done gets done.

GAZE: Then do it you bastard.

BEATY: I am. Look. I don't even move my hands.

I have subverted – the word? Eaten up – your police force, Ross. Unknown to you I have installed my own command structure. It has taken me many hours, many days, much concentration. But now – you can flap. Ross.

Ha! What are you? A pigeon, standing on my head, shitting down my back?

ROSS *and* BEATY *stare at each other.* GAZE *begins to turn away.*

Scene Fourteen

California, by a swimming pool.
MURGATROYD *lies in the sun in large*
floral swimming trunks. Three women CIA
AGENTS, *one in a jump suit, two in bikinis*
sit and lie by the pool. Each wears dark
glasses and has a two-way radio to hand.

MURGATROYD *has a trolley of exotic*
drinks beside him.

ROSS *is walking toward him. He stops.*

MURGATROYD: Hello Ross.

ROSS: Dennis.

MURGATROYD: Welcome to California.

Nothing from ROSS.

I heard you had fallen from favour. The
CIA brief me. Sweet boys and girls. They
maintain the fiction I am a king over the
water.

ROSS: Yes.

A silence.

MURGATROYD: So. You turn up by my
pool. What do you want? Go on a 'phone-
in? No, you're a more ambitious political
exile from Red Britannia. Nothing less
than the Johnny Carson Show for you.

He drinks. A radio crackles, one of the
AGENTS *lifts the radio and speaks into it.*
She catches ROSS's *eye and smiles.*

Don't look at them! They're CIA agents.
What did you think they were, my
whores?

(*He scoffs:*) Something funny's happened
to sex in America. Sex in America isn't
about sex at all.

He drinks. ROSS *looking away.*

ROSS: Your wife and your daughters.

MURGATROYD, *still, looks at his*
drink. A silence. Then he drains it. He
holds the glass out. An AGENT *comes*
and fills it.

MURGATROYD: What – ?

ROSS: They were in a police car. A mob set
about it. The car overturned and was
burned.

A silence.

MURGATROYD: Both my girls?

ROSS: Yes.

MURGATROYD: What – were they doing
in a police car?

ROSS: Arrested.

A silence.

MURGATROYD: For what?

ROSS *shrugs.*

ROSS: When you start a regiment of
Praetorian Guards, Special Troops, any
kind of Secret Police – they all clock on at
nine in the morning. And will find something to do in the working day. And, in
the end, run a country, whatever its
hallowed traditions. I know. I was their
chief.

MURGATROYD: So.

He nods.

It's all true. England is a killing ground.

Just like that.

Ha! Hearts of English oak? The valves
torn, filled with blood.

ROSS: We can sit here and be maudlin
about it. Or we can –

MURGATROYD: We can what?

ROSS: Restore freedom and democracy to
the British Isles.

MURGATROYD: Right. OK. Will do.
You and me –

He slams his drink down on the trolley. It
splashes.

Mr No-name Ross. You're here because
Beaty took your police force away. For
his own private use, no?

And you sail to America and go on TV to
cry 'Freedom' and 'Democracy'.

Go and wash your mouth out.

ROSS: Like you, with booze?

MURGATROYD: Yes, I am drinking
myself to death.

(*Slurring:*) Scientifically.

(*Cheerfully:*) It's going rather well. I'm
already getting heads out of the wall on
bad nights. Stalin. Dzerzhinskii. Beria.
Mine. My – children's.

He lifts his drink to the sun.

Booze in the California sun.

Light comes millions of miles to what? Splinter in alcohol into my eye.

And, in a few hours, when the planet turns – to hit the wet roofs of English towns.

Indifferent. Cold. Light.

ROSS: You disgust me.

MURGATROYD: Don't – that I can disgust you may give me hope. Dangerous, hope, for bastards like us. If anything's to be done –

A gesture.

'The people' will have to do it. And bleed, bleed.

The despised masses of all the rhetoric, eh?

That human wall we climbed up. Crampons in breasts, faces – and fell from.

Best we don't claw our way back. A kindness. You go and – disappear on the right-wing lecture circuit. Brutal middle-aged American women and college football players – they'll love you. I'll lie down here. Bottom of my bottle.

So let me alone. All of you. (*He waves at the* C.I.A. AGENTS. *They go off.*)

ROSS (*aside*): Six months later I went into a Los Angeles clinic. An inoperable tumour. A week before I died, they gave me the news – Henry Murgatroyd had been found, face down in his pool.

ROSS goes off. MURGATROYD *takes a bottle of vodka. He unscrews the cap and throws it away.*

MURGATROYD: Self-destruction. Oh the luxury of. By my pool of tears. Ha!

He drinks. The vodka runs down his shirt.

Over the sun. I –

BEATY *walks on the water of the pool.*

Walking on the water, Jack? Bloody typical. Do anything now, can you not. God, what gave you the right, the holier-than-thou right, to take everything in your hands, out-manouvre and out-do us all?

Don't go Jack! Invite me back. Give me

something to do. I'm a political animal, I can't live without it, the old cut and thrust, the mind-moil, the infighting, public life –

BEATY *walking on.*

You bastard. We were all friends, mucking in. Why did you have to go and spoil it for us all? We ought to have cut you down. Cut you –

He raises the vodka bottle and lunges at BEATY. *He steps into the pool and begins to fall.*

A blackout.

Scene Fifteen

An underground car-park. Carnations.
ROSE, CYGNA *and* JOAN.

JOAN, *crouched, making a low chant.*

JOAN: A spray-can a spray-can –

JOAN *laughs.*

CYGNA She'll come with police. Dogs and gas.

ROSE: She said there'd be no guards, there are no guards.

CYGNA: Why believe her?

ROSE: She's a woman.

JOAN: A slogan on a wall, a letter to *The Times.* Swing the duplicator's arm. A pamphlet, a pamphlet –

CYGNA: We must have nothing to do with her.

ROSE: Maybe these people are more tired than we know. And more frightened. Maybe they wither inside, become dry, a shell – which can be cracked, just by a touch.

CYGNA: Wishful thinking, sister.

JOAN: A heckle from the crowd, a stone thrown, a riot – an agitation, a boycott and a strike –

ROSE: I heard her.

JOAN: Millions who say 'No', millions who say 'No' –

ROSE: Come on.

They withdraw into the shadows. GAZE comes on, her arms full of flowers. She has not seen the three women.

GAZE: I'll put the flowers down.

A silence.

I'll put the flowers down.

She does so. She has a large torch.

Are you there?

A silence.

I'm in good faith. You must help.

ROSE, *from the shadows.*

ROSE: What do you want, bitch?

GAZE *whirls round.*

JOAN: One more conspiracy, one more assassination?

CYGNA: She wants us to kill her lover's policeman – and put in hers.

CYGNA *laughs.*

JOAN: Then someone will take power from her. A distant cousin, a lover she doesn't even remember.

GAZE: You've got to help me.

We've been driven into a hole, don't you see? Of having to rule by personal power. No leadership can stand that and be rational, be – humane. And not become distorted and cruel and –

A silence.

It is a matter of cruelty, you see. He can't govern, the cruelty's too much – there'll be disorder and resistance, reaction, we'll lose all we've gained –

A silence.

But we can put it all to rights. Curb powers. Hold shop floor elections.

CYGNA *laughs.*

Talk to community leaders –

The three women laugh.

Learn from past mistakes! Dismantle! Reform! Please –

They stop laughing.

There's a cruelty to yourself, too, you see. To yourself.

ROSE: You were right. We must have nothing to do with her.

ROSE, CYGNA *and* JOAN, *going.*

GAZE: It must be done.

CYGNA: What police state has ever destroyed itself? Said peace and given up?

ROSE: You were socialists and dreamt up tyranny. More dangerous than atomic waste. Better you be buried in glass. Deep. And pray the glass never cracks for twenty thousand years.

GAZE *weeps.*

CYGNA: The bitch weeps.

JOAN: Too late to wake up, Jenny.

ROSE, CYGNA *and* JOAN *have gone.*

GAZE switches on the torch.

GAZE: Where are you?

She flicks the beam about the walls.

Nothing. Underground, with flowers. Ha!

She kneels, spreading the flowers.

In a hole. A wide space? Room? A bunker? A field? A wood? The moon an electric bulb, a bulb the moon – sh. Sh, woman. What does it matter to you, my love? Me, my love. Let me talk to you, love. And you tell me little jokes and stories about who killed who. What have you done to yourself? I can't feel you, come down here, with me. In a room, in the grass, in a field, in a wood, in a cupboard, in a hole.

A light change to moonlight through moving branches.

Night sounds.

Scene Sixteen

Woodland. Night. JENNY GAZE *is scrabbling at the earth.*

JACK BEATY *comes on with a two-way radio.*

BEATY: Where?

The radio crackles.

In the trees, where?

He sees GAZE.

Oh God.

He watches her for a moment. Then he speaks into the radio.

All the cameras – all that spying, lying junk. Smash it.

The radio is silent.

You hear me? Not one of you look.

At her, like this.

He lets the radio hang from his wrist.

What are you doing up here, Jenny? Don't you know men – watch you everywhere in this wood?

She continues to scrabble in the earth.

Stop that! He's not buried here anymore. I had his body, him, it –

A gesture.

You always hated Bernard when he was alive.

She stops.

What have you taken?

GAZE: What's done is done.

BEATY: I can call a doctor, if you say.

GAZE *clutches her stomach.*

GAZE: Oh! Oh! Oh! Oh!

She stops, breathing heavily.

BEATY: Please, let me call them –

GAZE: Don't – be – sentimental.

BEATY: You're right. Good. I'll help you kill yourself. That way we'll be a modern couple to the end.

GAZE (*scoffs*): You'll have to leave me. I've got to fall asleep. The pills will – damage me, if I don't fall asleep.

BEATY: Oh Jenny, eat something – grass – be sick –

GAZE: You were always like a dog, frightened 'cos I'm strong.

BEATY (*low*): I loved you.

GAZE: You did not.

BEATY: How can you say that?

GAZE: You never fought me. Lovers must fight! If they don't, their bed's a nightmare, spooks and graves.

BEATY: Ah well, there was time. But –

GAZE: No, no, no, no you don't. Sentimental lover, bastard man. Tyrants make the countries they rule one vast panorama of their private lives. Well, look about you –

She laughs.

BEATY: Jenny –

GAZE: I must go to bed now. To bed, to bed, to bed, to bed.

She curls up and is still. BEATY waits, then stands and walks away. He stops. He speaks, low, into the radio.

BEATY: This area. No one comes near. No one sees.

Scene Seventeen

A bunker beneath Whitehall.

Above, in two blows, the clamour of riot and the smashing of steel doors.

BEATY, *alone.*

BEATY: I believed in so much, I wanted so much.

The clamour. He laughs.

What is my experience in Government? That authority is not loved. But, you want to make history, then be prepared to be a part of history. Even if that's a corpse in a ditch.

That is my contribution, my decisive contribution. A skeleton along the road, the shining road, the way forward.

He grips his fist.

To the future – the garden – the –

The clamour again. The ghosts of FEAST, GAZE, DUNN, MURGATROYD and ROSS appear in the shadows. He does not look at them.

But what do you expect? Someone must take it up. Authority, the banner, the will. You want universal justice, the common good? Well, the unjust, you know, aren't going to say 'Fine. Great. Here's our money and our houses and our banks, oilfields, all our revenues and power and very lives.' Oh no. You're going to have blood on your hands. You're going to have your dead. Eh, comrades?

People find it hard to believe in ideals, you see. Very hard. They'd rather believe in human nature – and that it's bad. Despite all the evidence, all the evidence to the contrary.

That we're good. And on a long high road. Ha! I don't believe in the conspiracy theory of history. I should know – I am a great conspirator.

So don't look for conscience, comrades. There is virtue in me. I did not corrupt it.

The ghosts begin to fade.

Take what analysis you fancy, off the shelf of the ideological supermarket. A Socialist Government that foundered on the usual rocks. A command economy.

Food prices held down artificially. With that, corruption. Black marketeering. And the people, sullen, angry, self-destructive. And government – blocked. In the mind, in the mind –

Gripping his fist.

Block-age. A blocked age. Rage, blocked.

But then! Every single hope of mankind is a bloody business, eh comrades? Eh?

The ghosts begin to leave.

So what does it matter, what does it matter? If good comes of it, the dead are forgotten. A century on and all will be well. All manner of things.

The figure of STALIN walks through the shadows.

A blackout as an alarm goes off. ROSE, CYGNA and JOAN, in the dark. They have torches.

ROSE: Switch that alarm off! Someone switch it off!

CYGNA: Must be on another circuit.

ROSE: Get it off –

The alarm stops.

Going right through me.

JOAN: The smell down here. Something burnt.

ROSE coughs.

CYGNA: Must be something still smouldering – ow!

JOAN: What?

CYGNA: S'all right, firebucket. (*She throws sand about.*) It's hot, it's hot. Hot.

JOAN: All this metal.

ROSE, coughing.

ROSE: It's electronics. Smashed up – careful, there may be something still live –

CYGNA's torch flicks over a dummy of a withered corpse in BEATY's chair.

CYGNA: Eh! It's him, it's him! He's all – burnt.

They burst into laughter.

It's the War Room. We've gone and blundered into the War Room.

They hold each other, laughing. Then a silence.

JOAN: Maybe he smashed it all up down here. All his telephones. Maybe he wanted people to pull it all to bits.

ROSE: What's it matter?

She gestures at the stage with her torch. She switches it out.

It's just underground. Let's get back up, and breathe.

CYGNA: I know. In the light. And celebrate and have a holiday – and swim, and talk, and think –

CYGNA and JOAN switch their torches out. A blackout and –

Epilogue

In the darkness, the crash of waves on a beach. Lights up. JENNY GAZE *and* JACK BEATY *are walking along a beach, well wrapped-up.* BEATY *has a lame leg and walks with a stick.*

BEATY: How – are you listening?

They stop.

How could a hit over the head, make a leg go like this?

GAZE: Well, you've talked about it.

She turns away.

BEATY: You don't think, when someone gets hit – 'bout injury.

GAZE: No.

A silence.

BEATY: All right! All right!

GAZE: I think we should just have this holiday, don't you. Since the Ward had a whip round to send us on it.

BEATY: Oh yes we are local heroes of a punch-up with the local fascists. Ha! First day it's not rained. Out of season two weeks the back end of Christmas. Thank you comrades.

GAZE: Don't – let's – moan.

BEATY: No.

GAZE: Cold comfort, love.

BEATY: I s'pose so.

I dreamt something, after the punch-up. When I was out. Funny, I feel it's the dream that's done my leg in, not the fight.

GAZE: Dream of what?

BEATY: Peace, funnily enough.

GAZE: I dreamt that, in a way.

BEATY: After a nightmare.

GAZE: Funny how we can't actually describe peace.

BEATY: You can bugger your leg up for it though.

GAZE: Yup.

She picks up a stone.

BEATY: But then, peace is not a personal matter, is it.

GAZE: No.

She is about to throw the stone. A blackout just before it leaves her hand.

A SHORT SHARP SHOCK!

A Short Sharp Shock! was first presented at the Theatre Royal, Stratford, East London, on 21 June 1980, with the following cast:

THE GOVERNMENT

MARGARET THATCHER	Gwen Taylor
SIR KEITH JOSEPH	Darlene Johnson
SIR GEOFFREY HOWE	Joanna Van Gyseghem
LORD PETER CARRINGTON	Maggie Steed
WILLIAM WHITELAW	Linda Spurrier
JIM PRIOR	Jane Wymark
NORMAN ST JOHN-STEVAS	Gil Brailey
NOTT	Alfred Molina
BIFFO	Alan Ford

IN BETWEEN

PIPKIN	Alfred Molina

THE GOVERNED

OLD MAN YULE	Godfrey Jackman
JEAN	Gil Brailey
MILLY STACKER	Mary Sheen
ARTHUR STACKER	Alan Ford

THE DEAD

THE GHOST OF AIREY NEAVE	Maggie Steed
THE GHOST OF LORD LOUIS MOUNTBATTEN OF BURMA	Jane Wymark

Other parts played by members of the company

Directed by Robert Walker
Designed by Sue Blane
Lighting by Jack Raby
Sound by Charles Wright

The Theatre Royal production of *A Short Sharp Shock!* transferred to the Royal Court Theatre, London on 16 July 1980.

The first amateur production of *A Short Sharp Shock!,* presented by Sheffield University Theatre Workshop at the University Drama Studio, was given simultaneously with the Theatre Royal opening. It was directed by John Bull and Louise Page.

ACT ONE

Scene One

A blackout.
In the background a constant, low chant of
'Out, Out'.
An effect. Six people with sparklers make the
letters of the words 'OUT NOW' for the
audience.
MILLY, *aside in the darkness.*

MILLY: 1974. Election night. Three day
week. Back in the good old days. The last
hours of power for a man called Ted
Heath –

A scream off-stage.

ARTHUR: Hang him!

MILLY: Shut up Arthur!

The low chant changes to 'Heath Out'.

(*Aside.*) The miners' strike brings the
Tory Government down.

A Prime Minister versus the people. The
people win.

ARTHUR: The revolution at last!

MILLY: Arthur – shut up!

ARTHUR: I'm going to light me bonfire
now! I got the petrol!

The 'OUT NOW' sparklers scatter.

An 'Ommph'. A bonfire blazes in the
centre of the stage.

Revealed are MILLY STACKER,
ARTHUR STACKER, JEAN YULE
and PIPKIN. JEAN is dressed as a
skinhead with a Sunderland F.C. shirt.
She is from Tyneside. ARTHUR wears a
miner's hat and a rusty, Civil War
breastplate.

MILLY (*aside*): Here we are, then.
Election night party. And we've all been
knocking on doors for Labour.

JEAN (*aside*): Not me, I'm not voting
Labour. I'm too political.

PIPKIN (*aside*): Pipkin. Junk shop
assistant.

JEAN (*aside*): Jean Yule. Day release. I
just live over the shop.

MILLY (*aside*): Milly Stacker. Woman with

a past. And that.

ARTHUR (*aside*): Arthur. Her husband.
And that. And we all work for Socialism!

PIPKIN (*aside*): In his junk shop!

ARTHUR (*aside*): Socialist memorabilia!
(*He thumps his breastplate.*) Breastplate
from the Civil war. Rusted with the blood
of King Charles the First! And now Ted
Heath! Two tyrants overthrown. (*He taps
the helmet.*) And a miner's helmet,
twentieth century.

JEAN (*aside*): I'm down here to hide from
all that.

A gesture at ARTHUR and MILLY.

London's just a great big forest to me.

ARTHUR: Ted Heath's on the TV!

MILLY (*aside*): You don't remember. In
1974 we all had hope.

ARTHUR: Even in the Parliamentary
Labour Party.

MILLY (*aside*): Even in Harold Wilson.

Everyone on stage spits.

ARTHUR: Heath's still bleeding on! Right!

ARTHUR *rushes off.*

PIPKIN: Oh no Arthur – the tube!

MILLY: Take me. Am I depressed? Never.
Have I seen Harold Wilson before?
Never. Have I been lifted up to the sky on
a cloud of farts before? Never.

PIPKIN: Cheer up Mrs Stacker.

He grabs JEAN's breasts from behind.

Brotherhood of Socialism.

JEAN *brings her heel up smartly into*
PIPKIN's *crotch. He yells and doubles*
up.

You'll regret that. I'm going to end up
Mayor of Southwark.

MILLY: Right little T. Dan Smith are we?

PIPKIN: That's what it's all about. Harold's
back in power. Now's my chance. The
thrusting young in the Labour Party.
Things are always going to get better!
(*Aside.*) We believed that once,
remember? Politics was about Wilson
versus Heath. Three falls or a knockout.
Big Daddy versus the Hooded Terror.

JEAN: I come down from Tyneside to get away from Socialism. You should hear my grandfather. All Marx and Match Girls and the Pilgrim's Progress. And I end up with you lot. I just want to go to The Talk of the Town every night.

PIPKIN, *a comb flashing*.

PIPKIN: Look, er, doll, I could lift a couple o' tickets – if you'd put a frock on.

JEAN *takes the comb and breaks it in half, delicately*.

MILLY: Oh the young.

ARTHUR *staggers on with a TV set*.

ARTHUR: I'm sick of all this rubbish on TV!

PIPKIN: Don't matter – only black and white, in't it –

ARTHUR: Can you hear me in there, Ted? Trying to take over my brain? Tell me who governs Britain?

(*Aside.*) With a great wrench of his body he heaves the TV set onto the bonfire.

He does so.

PIPKIN, *hiding behind* JEAN.

PIPKIN: The tube! The tube'll go up!

ARTHUR: Spontaneous expression of Revolutionary Joy. That's all.

MILLY: Right! Now we burnt Ted Heath alive, what shall we do? Official Labour Party knees-up? Go and be thanked by the right-wing pig we knocked on doors for? And come the rosy morn, Downing Street and Harold Wilson under the cameras, announcing the Workers' State.

PIPKIN: I've seen a Workers' State. Bulgaria. Great. Lovely beaches. Duty-free shop, cashmere sweaters. I've seen it.

MILLY: We been to Bulgaria, haven't we Arthur? (*To* JEAN:) He got seduced by a Secret Policeman, disguised as a woman.

ARTHUR (*furious*): They see things differently over there!

MILLY: The slap and tickle.

JEAN (*to* PIPKIN): Milly left the Communist Party 'cos of Hungary. (*To* MILLY:) Didn't you Pet.

PIPKIN: Poor old sod.

MILLY (*fiercely*): Don't worry about me. Worry about you, Pipkin, in five years time. (*To* JEAN:) You too girl. With or without hair.

PIPKIN: I've got a lot of confidence. Lot of sharp people in Labour. These people trickle down the back of my neck and give me a warm feeling. Reg Prentice. Shirley Williams. John Stonehouse. They'll look after go-getters like me, like a bat out of nowhere.

MILLY (*to* JEAN): These people will give you nothing. I've sat on toilets next to these people. Labour Party conferences, Brighton, Blackpool, Skegg-bloody-ness.

ARTHUR: Don't be cynical, don't let's always be cynical. Ted Heath's a ruin, he's been on pills for three nights. The miners! A man who works has power. At last we know. The miners proved it! I'm gonna let the fireworks off!

ARTHUR *busies himself*.

JEAN: I don't see myself in anything you say. 'A man who works'? On the whole – one thing and another – I don't want to be a man.

PIPKIN: See me straight, you won't have to work either. Just bring up the kids.

JEAN *gives* PIPKIN *a kidney punch*.

MILLY (*aside*): So Arthur's wrong 'cos he thinks he's in an heroic age, but he's not. And Pipkin's wrong, a little baby sting-ray putting his faith in killer whales and Jean –

JEAN (*aside*): I'm in my rejections phase. But I'm biding my time.

MILLY (*aside*): And me, Milly? I stand here in 1974 and try to think ahead. The Tory Party? Ted Heath in a bath with his wrists cut. The assassins, for leader, get a real right-wing nutter. Out of the slime. And no one will ever vote for them again. And the Labour Party? However small the majority in Parliament, they'll remember who put them there – and change. And we'll live in dignity. Industrial democracy. Dignity. Hope out of cynicism, you see.

JEAN: Hope springs eternal. You sound like my grandad.

ARTHUR' I've dropped my lighter in the

firework box!

Bangs. Firework effects. PIPKIN, *his arms raised above his head.*

PIPKIN: I want to be a great man! A great man! A great man!

Scene Two

AIREY NEAVE *wanders on. He is dressed plainly in a suit. He is smiling. He sniffs.*

NEAVE: Great man? Great man?

Good evening. I'm Airey Neave. The man who got Margaret Thatcher power. Alive and well in 1974.

You heard that bit about me in Colditz. So I won't go on about that. But did you know I was wounded four inches from the heart in Calais? Flesh wound. Damn lucky to be alive. There was a machine gun behind the net curtains. When I came round the ambulance smelt of cabbages.

He sniffs.

World's been like that ever since. See, my character was formed in simple, bloody times. Made me a good man –

A wintery smile.

With some violent opinions. Like, well – vigilantes, arm the householders – 1974. Two, the Labour Party are Nazis – 1978.

That's me. Now would you all please – sit up! Shoulders straight! No fainting! Pay attention to HOW MARGARET THATCHER CAME TO POWER, or – how the old Tory Party gave birth to a monster.

Once upon a time there was a man called Edward Heath.

ARTHUR (*a shout, off*): Hang him!

MILLY (*off*): Shut up Arthur!

NEAVE: Don't worry, Heath will not appear tonight. A failed Tory is a leper.

Heath has lost. The elder Tories gather behind closed doors. Come with me to a vast estate in Scotland purple with heather. To meet, in a vast ancestral wine cellar –

NEAVE *blows a party whizzer.* LORD ALEC HOME *comes on. He is loaded with guns and bandoliers. He gets tangled with them.*

Lord Alec Home. The High Priest of High Toryism. He is a nice man who likes to kill little birds.

ALEC: You can pay a bird no better compliment than by killing it.

NEAVE (*pointing at* ALEC's *head*): This man was Prime Minister from November 1963 to October 1964. He lost a General Election to Harold Wilson.

They spit.

Just like Heath.

ARTHUR (*off*): Hang him!

NEAVE: But Alec withdrew gracefully from the Leadership of the Party. After a campaign of personal vilification by some supporters of –

ALEC: What I can never understand about Edward, is why – on the night I resigned – he went to see *Macbeth*.

LORD PETER THORNEYCROFT *comes on. Twenty pound notes flutter from his pockets, his sleeves when he waves his arms, his shirt when he scratches himself. He is accompanied by a* CHAUFFEUR. CHAUFFEUR *drinks from an old wine bottle, from which cobwebs and big spiders dangle.*

NEAVE (*aside*): Enter another forgotten man.

He blows a party whizzer.

Lord Peter Thorneycroft.

THORNEYCROFT (*aside*): Driven here all night in my Daimler. In a storm. And a filthy temper. I'm not the wealthy man people think I am. It's all on paper.

CHAUFFEUR (*aside*): So are ten pound notes.

THORNEYCROFT (*shaking money away from him*): Damn! Blast!

My God, Alec. There's a hole all the way up to your roof. You can see the sky.

ALEC: Yes. People don't understand how poor the very rich are.

CHAUFFEUR: It's all soup kitchens and caviar round here.

THORNEYCROFT: There're birds going over –

ALEC: Oh jolly.

He points two guns upwards.

Bang.

Many dead birds fall down on the stage.

ALEC: Point, fetch, carry, retrieve, down, stay, heel –

THORNEYCROFT: Alec, please. The Tory Party needs your weight and your mind.

ALEC (*twitish*): Oh!

THORNEYCROFT: Heath must go.

ALEC: Easy-peasy. Re-arrange the rules when we re-elect the Party Leader. All you do is, on the first ballot – oh no. Not sporting.

THORNEYCROFT: It's time to take out the axe and the block –

NEAVE (*aside*): Thorneycroft. Chairman of Trust House Forte. Chairman of Pye. Chairman of Pirelli.

THORNEYCROFT: Disembowel Ted Heath.

NEAVE: And director of Securicor.

ALEC: Oh good, shenanigans.

THORNEYCROFT: To speak the truth – or a version of it –

ALEC: Yes, let's not get our brains in a tizzle –

THORNEYCROFT: Do you or do you not want – revenge?

ALEC: Boot Ted Heath out of the Leadership?

THORNEYCROFT: Like he booted you.

ALEC: An eyeball for an eyeball. Alec's revenge.

He squawks.

Let me have a crisis of conscience about that.

A silence. THORNEYCROFT *looks at his watch, bad-temperedly.*

Well?

I'm waiting for my years of breeding to tell.

THORNEYCROFT: For God's sake Alec, come on. We're the pillars of the Tory Party. Of the wealth of England – are we going to be pulled down? As they smash up statues in a banana republic? So miners can use your head and my head for pumice stones in the pithead baths – I mean why isn't the man married? It's not Tory.

Slipped his cabinet with self-made manikins. Walker, Jim Prior. Would Wilson have had his balls blacked by a pack of coal heavers?

ALEC *jerks suddenly.*

ALEC: Oh it's gone away.

THORNEYCROFT: What?

ALEC: My conscience. Mind you, I am going to be an elder statesman about this and not get personally involved.

(*Suddenly manic.*) I'm just going to cut the bastard down.

Bang!

The CHAUFFER *drops the bottle, doubling over and clutching his stomach. He staggers about unnoticed.*

CHAUFFEUR: Perils of being in service. They used to have your wife on your wedding-night too.

He collapses.

ALEC: right, who shall we have instead? Willie Whitelaw. He's one of us.

THORNEYCROFT: Creepy-crawlie. Second-rate mind. Give him a chair and he wouldn't see it.

CHAUFFEUR: My stomach!

ALEC: Reggie Maudling?

THORNEYCROFT: Nice man. But we're cleaning the party up.

CHAUFFEUR: It's falling out!

THORNEYCROFT: The nation's gone soft. It's not up to the rich to look after the weak. I mean, what do the poor want money for, to wipe their bums?

He flaps his arms. Money flies.

NEAVE (*aside*): Peter Thorneycroft was thrown out of the Cabinet by Harold Macmillan in 1957 because of his aggressive monetarist views on public spending. With him went his Junior Minister, Enoch Powell.

A cuckoo calls.

THORNEYCROFT: I have waited years! I've gone green on the insides.

CHAUFFEUR: I voted for these people!

He collapses.

THORNEYCROFT: We need a strong man! To let the people free!

ALEC (*horrified*): The people? What people, where –

THORNEYCROFT: I mean men like us you fool.

ALEC, *thinking.*

ALEC: Someone strong, someone brainy, someone a bit frightening –

They look at each other.

THORNEYCROFT ⎱
ALEC: ⎰ Keith Joseph

THORNEYCROFT: You've shot my driver. How am I going to get home?

ALEC: Stay to dinner. (*Picking up and peering at a bird.*) It's jugged hare.

They are off.

CHAUFFEUR: Help!

NEAVE: Get off, lad. You're only maimed.

CHAUFFEUR: Sorry sir.

The CHAUFFEUR *gets up and walks off.*

NEAVE (*aside*): Ladies and gentlemen, Sir Keith Joseph. Sir Keith has kindly come here tonight to explain he isn't mad. He will summarise an unusually interesting speech he gave on social policy on the 19th October, 1974. It was his bid for the Leadership of the Tory Party.

SIR KEITH JOSEPH *comes on. He speaks into a microphone.*

KEITH: Good evening. It's not true I want to gas people. Or kill them in any way. I just don't want so many people to get born.

Oh, if only I could make myself clear to ordinary people.

I'm not talking about all of you not getting born.

I'm not talking about that at all.

A silence.

I'm talking about contraceptives.

I'll begin again. There are a lot of people in this country who through no fault of their own are working-class. I do hope this applies to no one here tonight.

He takes a deep breath.

I mean I don't call anyone working-class. I find that patronizing. I talk about people who are in social classes 4 and 5. Sadly. The poor souls. You will never get me to say anything else but that it is a very cruel world. And if working-class women, women from social classes 4 and 5 did not have so many children there would be far fewer of them. And their wretched spawn who fill up the prisons, denizens of borstals, hostels for drifters and loony bins.

Look, this line of thought is a torment to me.

Increasing numbers of totally uneducated babies are being born every day. The balance of our stock is threatened. Too many cooks and coalminers and shop-girls are spoiling the nation's broth. Too many ill-fitted women are giving birth.

We must see that they are better fitted. If their morals are slipping it is essential that their coils do not.

You understand me.

I don't want them to eat cake. I just want them to eat contraceptives and decrease. Then they wouldn't be unemployed, they wouldn't be degraded, because they wouldn't be there.

What? What? Yes I do hear voices telling me I should be leader of the Tory Party. If you think a man with a mind like mine cannot have power in this country you are gravely mistaken.

We must remoralise the nation. We must dismantle a hundred and fifty years of culture, mass education, bitter, bitter Dead Sea fruit. We must unteach and unlearn. We must make a start by decreasing the fertility of working – of certain men and women.

He hears voices.

What? What?

He hides his face.

Ooooooh! Why do I have to use words, why can't I just give you my brain?

A trick magician's saw shoots out from his hand. He begins to saw his head off. A loud sawing noise, off.

NEAVE: Keith – Keith – Keith –

He stops sawing.

KEITH: Hello.

NEAVE: Your speech didn't go down very well with the Tory Party bosses. They're afraid if you were Leader, people wouldn't vote for us.

KEITH: In the name of everything sane, why not?

NEAVE: Because you don't know what every Tory Leader must know.

KEITH: What?

NEAVE: You never say working-class in public.

KEITH: I'm sorry. I must be sick. At least I think I think I must.

NEAVE: No, Keith –

KEITH: I'll go away. I'll lock myself in a small cupboard. Somewhere dark and punishing. And come out in two days time and tell you what I think of myself.

He howls with tears.

NEAVE: And Keith came out of his cupboard.

KEITH: I am not a giant. You will need a giant for the struggle ahead of you. I will not stand for the leadership of the Tory party.

He begins to sink, on a trap, into the stage. The finger shoots up.

People have got to suffer. I say to the unemployed, 'There is no hope'. It would be cruel of me to say otherwise. Why do they call me the Mad Monk? Why do they call me His Insanity?

He is gone, weeping.

NEAVE (*aside*): And now, the Tories in Parliament. The Party of gentlemen – and a few women.

Leaderless.

An effect.
240 dummies in suits, the fat, the thin and the thuggish in chinless wonder masks, are flown in fast and jerk, bouncing there, filling the stage.

The sound of dogs barking and yapping.

Actors in similar suits and masks, as TORY MPs, run in among the dummies cracking whips.

They quieten down. The whips stop. A sense of suspicion comes over the TORY MPs.

TORY MPs: Grrr. Grrr. Woof, woof.

They sniff each other.

The three HEATHITES *in Heath masks with whips run out of the ruck. They crack their whips around* NEAVE.

1ST HEATHITE: Who are you –

NEAVE: Airey Neave.

2ND HEATHITE: Airey? Airey who –

NEAVE: The Member for Abingdon.

3RD HEATHITE: We're Ted's men, Airey –

2ND HEATHITE: Who are you pushing for Leader, Airey –

1ST HEATHITE: Willie Whitelaw –

They laugh and crack whips.

2ND HEATHITE: Maudling –

3RD HEATHITE: Fatty –

They roar and crack whips.

1ST HEATHITE: He wants to bring Enoch back from Ireland –

A cuckoo calls.

NEAVE: Actually, I'm mildly interested in Edward Du Cann –

1ST HEATHITE: Woof –

The 1ST HEATHITE *springs at* NEAVE's *calf and chews it.*

2ND HEATHITE: Du Cann –

3RD HEATHITE: The Lonrho Banker –

2ND HEATHITE: Du Cann's spreadng lies about Ted you know, saying no one likes him – and they do –

You do, don't you Airey – ?

3RD HEATHITE: You'd better –

2ND HEATHITE: Du Cann's business interests –

3RD HEATHITE: The TUC's got a file on Du Cann –

2ND HEATHITE: Sniffy very sniffy –

3RD HEATHITE: If he gets the Leadership it will all come out, accidentally –

NEAVE: You mean Ted Heath's got a file on Du Cann –

The 2ND *and* 3RD HEATHITES *wag their fingers, making the back-bench jeering sound with dog overtones.*

HEATHITES: Ah ah, woof woof, ah –

2ND HEATHITE: Ted Heath doesn't know we're talking to you.

1ST HEATHITE: But there's a 'phone in his flat –

Wagging fingers.

3RD HEATHITE: Ted Heath runs the party machine –

2ND HEATHITE: And, Airey, you wouldn't want the party machine, in lovely Abingdon, to dump you –

HEATHITES: Ah ah, woof woof, ah –

NEAVE: My God! Dirty tricks in the Conservative and Unionist Party? I am amazed. Isn't this the party of loyalty and trust?

1ST HEATHITE: So you're Ted's friend now, Airey –

2ND HEATHITE: He likes you very much –

3RD HEATHITE: Everybody's happy.

A silence.

1ST HEATHITE: We're going to have an election for Leader. And woops! No one dare stand against Ted, dare they Airey? Next!

Desolate howls from the Party. The three HEATHITES *tiptoe back into the ruck, patting dummies, booting them occasionally. The lights dim over the massed Tory Party.*

NEAVE: Are ideals dead? In these drizzling times who will hold the umbrella over Britain? I think it's time for an Officer to act.

From the Tory Party – a desultory 'Auld Lang Syne' and hiccups.

New Year's Eve, 1974.

Airey Neave has a little secret dinner with Margaret Thatcher.

Resembling the real Margaret Thatcher as closely as possible MARGARET THATCHER *rises on a trap, seated at a small dinner-table.*

NEAVE *puts a party hat on.*

(*Aside.*) Margaret has come.

He blows a party squeaker.

MARGARET: I always wanted to be the first woman Chancellor of the Exchequer. And model myself on Dennis Healey.

But – put your hand on the table and let me touch it, in a feminine manner –

NEAVE *puts his hand on the table. She clamps her hand down on his. He squeaks.*

There never will be a woman Prime Minister in my time.

Head on one side.

Will there, Airey?

NEAVE: You could be Leader of the Tory Party and the next Prime Minister. Given the right tactics. The right campaign. Run by a man like me. I was an Army Intelligence Officer in the war.

MARGARET, *one hand still clamping his to the table, extends a fork with food on it.*

MARGARET: Tit-bit?

NEAVE: I mean – I want nothing for myself.

MARGARET: Open!

She pops food in his mouth.

NEAVE (*his mouth full*): Be my crusade Margaret –

MARGARET: I have only the body of a weak and feeble woman.

NEAVE: But –

He swallows.

Queen Elizabeth the First said that!

MARGARET (*steely*): I know. I have decided to be a great man.

NEAVE: Tell me your ideals, Margaret. (*Aside.*) I'm testing her.

MARGARET: You know, Keith and I, poor Keith, do have something in common, no matter what you say about us. We both have no toes.

(*Earnestly.*) He's so very, very right you

see. People are going to have to suffer.

NEAVE: I've waited years to hear someone say that!

MARGARET: Politicians are either healers or warriors. I'm a warrior.

Moral cripples just have to go to the wall.

NEAVE: Oh Margaret. You're talking about the Trade Unions. How wonderful.

MARGARET: Keith always says – 'The lean king is eating the healthy cows'.

NEAVE: Er – what does he mean?

MARGARET (*steely*): Isn't it obvious?

NEAVE: Yes, yes of course –

MARGARET: Soc – ial – ism, Airey. The Welfare State. To Keith and I, Mr Macmillan was a Communist.

NEAVE: Harold Macmillan? A double agent?

MARGARET: We must go far, far, far to the right.

NEAVE: The dead, oh the dead, they did not die in vain.

(*Aside.*) She's passed my test.

MARGARET: How do we win on the first ballot?

NEAVE: Two people have fixed it, Alec and Ted. Alec by changing the rules, Ted by being horrible to everyone.

He blows his squeaker. MARGARET *taps him on his head with her fork.*

MARGARET: We shan't be petty, Airey. or cafish. We'll just make sure Ted Heath will never rise again.

NEAVE (*leaps up*): Let's get cracking! I'll recruit spies.

MARGARET: No need. Just send every backbencher round to me and I'll attend to them – alone.

NEAVE (*aside*): What does she mean? Seduction? Fingernails?

MARGARET: Everything will go very nicely, but you'll tell everyone it's going badly.

NEAVE (*pants like a dog*): Yes Margaret. (*Pants. He darkens.*) But – when Heath's filleted on the first ballot the rest will come in, Prior, Whitelaw, Howe –

MARGARET: Theirs is the coward's charter. She who dares wins.

NEAVE: Margaret, oh. You're the bravest man in the Tory Party.

MARGARET: Pudding?

She stuffs pudding in his mouth with the fork. She offers a cheek.

Kiss.

He kisses her cheek, his mouth full of food. She stands up and smoothes herself as the table disappears. She smiles at the audience, goes out. The lights rise on the ranks of TORY MPs.

And agitation begins in the ranks of dummies. The masked actors peep out from among them. Dummies sway. NEAVE turns to them, arms outstetched.

NEAVE: My Right Honourable Friends, fellow Conservatives – let Maggie save Britain.

The dummies jerk up and down, dancing to crescending barks which blast into 'Well hullo Maggie', to the tune of 'Hullo Dolly'. MARGARET dances on. KEITH and THORNEYCROFT run in from opposite sides with big bunches of flowers. She offers each a cheek for a kiss and throws the flowers to NEAVE. She raises both hands in a characteristic gesture of triumph. At once, silence.

MARGARET: Thank you Peter. You have power again. You're Chairman of the Party. Purge it.

Thank you Keith, you'll always have my ear.

She goes to the microphone.

A new age of self-interest has begun.

Scene Three

The shop. A stack of Trade Union banners, unfurled. An old printing press (William Morris). Piles and piles of books, one a stack of 'Left Book Club' volumes with orange covers. Posters from the British nineteenth century, the Spanish Civil War, the Paris Commune, Russia 1917-22. Piles of weapons going back to the seventeenth century. Spools of film, a projector, a home movie screen. A section of railings, with a shop window dummy in 1910 women's clothes chained to the railings, a placard – 'WOMEN UNITE' and an SPG shield against the railings.

PIPKIN, MILLY and JEAN before a portable television set.

MILLY is deep in newspapers, holding them up before her. She is a speedy reader – she floats papers away. JEAN has a baby at her breast. She has long hair.

PIPKIN (*aside*): 1979. Another General Election. What have you missed? Five years of Labour and my youth.

JEAN (*aside*): Missed my glamorous life in London. Growing my hair. Guru Maharadji. Levitating at the Palace of Peace, East Dulwich. Giving that up. Sid Vicious. Giving that up. And that was the seventies for me. Leadership syndrome. (*To* PIPKIN:) But found my place in the grand design, didn't I Pipkin? Married to you.

PIPKIN: Let me alone! Let me think! Go and wash up! Where are my underpants! I've got a headache!

JEAN: Just 'cos I was into love for a month and you were a feminist fellow-traveller.

PIPKIN: I'm going down the marriage guidance!

JEAN: I'm going down the pub.

PIPKIN: Not with her! She's got burps!

JEAN: Grandad, on the phone, said my marriage is going to pot because of Jim Callaghan.

PIPKIN: Your Grandad. Reversed the charges again didn't he! From Newcastle-upon-Tyne –

JEAN: Grandad says the Government is frightened to death of the future. That's why our marriage is a hearse.

PIPKIN: Oh thank you, thank you Grandad.

MILLY: What?

MILLY *lowers a newspaper. She is wearing big earplugs.*

I am wearing earplugs so I can think politically.

MILLY's *paper up then down at once.*

She won't get in. She can't get in. People aren't fools.

MILLY's *paper up.*

JEAN: Grandad says it's stupid of us to go knocking doors, canvassing for Labour. Politicians like Callaghan and Healey warm their brown soup over other people's fire.

MILLY: If there's a swing to the Tories of 4.7 –

MILLY's *paper down.*

She won't get in. She can't get in. What's her policy? Cut tax for the rich and give the coppers bigger boots. A new age of self-interest? People aren't slugs. Each under his own stone.

ARTHUR *staggers on, drunk.*

ARTHUR: I want the televishun shet.

JEAN: Milly –

MILLY *doesn't move.* PIPKIN, *backing away.*

PIPKIN: The tube – don't –

ARTHUR (*aside*): I am now a drunk. During the Labour Government of 1974 to 1979 I have collapsed into Left-wing peshimism and deshpair. Every night Dennis Healey comes and sits on my chest – and I drink to make him go away.

He picks up the television set.

(*Aside.*) I voted for the Ecology Party. I want to see how they got on.

He staggers off with the television set. MILLY *lowers the paper.*

JEAN, *mouthing 'Arthur'.*

MILLY (*aside*): He's got himself a green-house. He's trying to grow soya beans. And develop a new tomato that will feed the world. Unfortunately, 'cos of his drinking, he keeps on walking through the glass.

JEAN: Why do you put up with him?

MILLY (*fiercely*): And don't ask me why I put up with him. He's a war hero. Arthur turned down the VC. 1945, if Churchill had got in, he was all set to be a partisan in the Cotswolds. Arthur's always seen himself as a one man guerrilla unit. He's just lost his way in the seventies a bit, that's all.

MILLY, *a paper up. It's the 'Guardian'. Paper down at once.*

Who is this bloody man in this bog roll, Peter Jenkins? On the one hand, on the other, up my arse and off the top of my head –

She pokes the paper.

All these 'Reasonable men'! The thundering hooves of sheep rushing to the right.

MILLY, *another paper up.*

PIPKIN: That kid's got pneumonia.

JEAN: You what?

PIPKIN: Canvassing with a baby on your tit.

JEAN: Out of the mouths –

PIPKIN: All right! I know I'm being shitty. Can we all agree, tonight I'm being shitty.

JEAN: We are suffering the symptoms of our masters' disease.

MILLY, *paper down. She takes her earplugs out.*

MILLY: Right! Election party.

JEAN: Oh great. Rip the lagers open.

MILLY: Yeah! The frozen rat piss.

A crash off-stage.

ARTHUR *comes on, half the side of a greenhouse, glass broken, with a tangle of tomato plants, around his head and arms.*

ARTHUR: Thatcher. Thatcher.

MILLY: Oh Arthur, what's the matter?

ARTHUR: The first reshult.

He looks about him. He makes a great effort.

The computer predicts – a Conslurative Government hash won the Generally

Elecshun of nineteen sheventy-nine.

He collapses, sitting down.

A silence.

Then MILLY *pours lager over her head.*

Oh nooo, yearsh of it, yearsh and yearsh and yearsh – I wash in Cable Street. Know what that wash, Pipkin?

PIPKIN: No.

ARTHUR (*angrily*): What have you heard of? Civil War in Spain?

PIPKIN (*angrily*): Real Madrid?

ARTHUR: Jarrow March?

PIPKIN: Song, weren't it? Georgie Fame. No I tell a lie – Alan Price.

ARTHUR: God the generations. Have we gotta learn it, live it, do it – over and over again? Don't anyone remember the namesh? Don't we know our dead anymore?

PIPKIN: They stuck me in concrete up to my knees, that's all!

GRETA, *a woman neighbour, comes on.*

JEAN: Oh hello Greta.

GRETA: Now you gone and down it!

JEAN: What, Greta?

GRETA: Don't talk to me! I've heard you in here! Political lot! Arguing! Posters up in the windows! Well – you gone and down it now.

JEAN: Done what?

GRETA *pointing at the baby.*

GRETA: Oh the poor little mite. You let that fart in! That Thatcher!

JEAN: We're Labour, Greta –

GRETA: She's a fucking fart! Get her out!

JEAN: Milly I'll lose my mind!

GRETA: The fart!

JEAN: You voted for –

GRETA: Vote? What's voting to to do with it? I haven't got time to vote! I hid upstairs when the car came round. First time I set eyes on her I knew she was a fart. Get rid of her! Get her out! Roll her flat! What they do in Africa do that with her! Ant-hills! Who does the fart think

she is, the Queen?

JEAN: We're workers for the Labour Party!

GRETA: And it's down to you! You're to blame! Get rid of that woman! I've told you why! She's a fucking fart!

GRETA *goes off fast.*

MILLY: The world's changed. Arthur? Feel it?

ARTHUR: Where's – a – gin?

MILLY: They can't. They can't. They can't. It's an insult to women. She's Enoch Powell in skirts.

Give me me earplugs! I got to think!

She puts the earplugs in, holding her head.

I can hear her voice. Like a siren in the war. What's she saying? All the muck spitting out of her – double-talk and bile. 'Freedom of the Individual' meaning hate your neighbour – and Keith Joseph, 'The balance of our stock is threatened.'

Margaret Hilda Thatcher is the ball on the end of a demolition crane, crashing into everything that's decent in my country. Freedom? Free choice? Community groups? Unions? Nurseries? They'll pulverise the lot. Wherever people gather together there'll be a hole. We'll be in a great big sludge tank. Sinking free.

Hard-line, vicious, loony, right-wing cant. Know who their saint is? Adam Smith. What did he cause? The Irish Famine. So why? What the hell is History doing – landing Britain with this lot now? What has Margaret Hilda Thatcher sniffed out that we all missed?

Click.

The coming panic.

The wealth of nations is dribbling away. Thirty years, we thought – things will always get better, Christmas trees in the North Sea. We never looked further than the wheel of our Ford Capri, or our plate of roast lamb on Sunday. All the Western world is getting poorer. And tonight – Thatcher and the New Right are cornering the supply. Oh, the lady is a great class warrior. They've got to smash down now before we get the right slogans. They'll cordon us off. Shanty towns. South London? Sludge tank. The streets are stinking. When you smash anger you get a smell like fear.

All right Thatcher. The world is poor. So we all get poorer. Above all the rich.

And how do we do that, eh? How do we get her? How?

Still!

She claps her hands.

Heroic times have just begun.

PIPKIN: I voted for Mrs T.

A silence, all staring at him.

ARTHUR: I'll kill him! Let me kill him now! I'll kill him!

PIPKIN: Why not? Slice me up. See if I bleed. See, I been reading a lot of Tory literature. The past three weeks I wasn't canvassing for your lot. At all.

I've joined the Tory Party.

See, I'm going to be an entrepreneur.

See, I've got a pamphlet here written by Keith Joseph. If you are not prejudiced, you will read it.

MILLY: My God. He's gone mad.

JEAN: No, he's just a shit. Aren't you Pipkin, pet.

PIPKIN *ignores that.*

PIPKIN: You see, I got talent. And what you all don't realise is, all this, the last five, ten, thirty years – no good.

MILLY: We know it! So. That's why – Pipkin!

PIPKIN: No. It's tooth and claw. Nasty, brutish and short.

MILLY: What? What is?

PIPKIN: Human nature.

JEAN: What do you know about human nature?

PIPKIN, *wierdly calm.*

PIPKIN: Sir Keith says we're not in the Garden of Eden anymore. And, Milly, if you read between the lines – which you can do if you're intelligent –

MILLY: Which you are?

PIPKIN: Sir Keith has told me. Pipkin is a talented young man, he's got the right to

do anything he can get his hands on. Tooth and claw. And anything that gets in Pipkin's way is tyranny.

Free enterprise. That kid! Put her on the game. Or let her be a chimney sweep. Like in the nineteenth century. She's got talent. End up the queen of chimney brushes or a Mayfair madam. Keeping us all in our old age.

Throw me out then, Doll.

Right. I think I'll go to Downing Street. See Maggie ride up on her white charger.

JEAN: Don't slip on her horse-shit.

ARTHUR: He wouldn't slip, he'd merge.

PIPKIN: See you at the divorce then, Doll.

PIPKIN *goes off.*

JEAN: Oh you old campaigners. Who's going to look after you? The young aren't. Milly – help me get Arthur up.

MILLY: No. (*To* ARTHUR:) Stand up yourself. (*To* JEAN:) If he can't there's no hope.

JEAN: Don't you need me? Then I'm going. Out of London. Out of this pit.

JEAN *and the baby go off slowly.*

MILLY: You're not really dead are you, Arthur?

ARTHUR *bounces up.*

ARTHUR: Right! That's me post-election depression done. I'm going to close down my shop. Socialist memorabilia goodbye. I'm going to get into blatantly vicious and unfair propaganda. I'll open a stall and sell badges and violent posters.

MILLY: Ah! Thatcher's days are numbered.

ARTHUR: Too right. Never say die.

MILLY: Snap.

Blackout

Explosion

Scene Four

An afterlife.
A wind-machine off.
NEAVE *comes on, dressed as before,*
carrying a severed, bloodstained arm.

NEAVE: Now I am the Ghost of Airey Neave. I hear them say I was blown apart by a bomb in the House of Commons carpark on the 30th March, 1979, because of the British presence in Ireland.

I cite myself.

As a military man, I know young lads will rise up against tyranny and kill their oppressor. Now young men have risen up and killed me.

I am confused.

I do not understand why I am dead.

It is August 27th at Crossmaglen, in Northern Ireland.

The ghost of LORD LOUIS MOUNTBATTEN *comes on in full naval uniform. He carries a severed bloodstained arm.*

MOUNTBATTEN (*to* NEAVE): Good afternoon. I'm Dicky Mountbatten.

NEAVE: Oh. Good afternoon, Sir.

MOUNTBATTEN: Enjoyed that book of yours about war crimes.

NEAVE: Oh. Thank you Sir.

MOUNTBATTEN: How do you think Maggie's getting on, then?

NEAVE: I think it's not quite going to plan, Sir.

A British Army SQUADIE *comes on with a bucket marked 'Unknown Soldier'. He picks up debris from the floor.*

MOUNTBATTEN: Hard man on Ireland weren't you? Going to get the job.

NEAVE: Bloody Ireland! No British statesman ever did his reputation good in Ireland.

MARGARET THATCHER *comes on in a flak jacket. She poses in a tank, hair windswept, for unseen photographers.*

MOUNTBATTEN: Maggie. She's on walkabout in Ulster.

NEAVE *goes up to talk to her.*

MOUNTBATTEN: Waving the flag.

NEAVE: Margaret, it's Airey!

She doesn't know he's there.

What are you doing here? Why aren't you in England? Don't go on publicity stunts – save the Nation. You haven't sold off British Rail! You haven't bashed the unions to bits yet!

Go home!

Go home!

MOUNTBATTEN: You don't understand old man. Troops!

When I was alive back in the days of Harold Wilson –

MARGARET *and the* SQUADIE *spit.*
They look at each other, startled.

I went to a meeting of some top chaps. And some from the *Daily Mirror*. And saw we'd end up needing troops in English streets. Get the people out the people voted in.

Then some Wilsonite called Solly Zuckerman said 'This is rank treason Dicky. I'm not staying and nor should you.' And he walked out. I stayed.

Keep the troops happy! It's all part of the same thing.

NEAVE: Margaret, you know not what you do.

MOUNTBATTEN: Woman's a Machiavelli among the teacups I'd have thought. Don't worry old man. You have not died in vain. The British dead in Ireland are the jewels in her crown. Give her five years. All the time in the world. She'll bring the country to heel yet.

NEAVE: You think that, Sir?

MOUNTBATTEN (*cheerfully*): Oh the Royal Family doesn't have any opinions on anything. Officially. We're just there to be killed – if they can get to us.

The wind machine.

ALBION YULE, *an Old Man, comes on. He has a long white beard and an injured foot, which turns inward. He carries a big stick. He waves the stick.*

OLD MAN: Spirits of the air, be gone!

NEAVE *and* MOUNTBATTEN *move*

away backwards.

MOUNTBATTEN: Hey! We're being wafted away –

NEAVE: Margaret –

MOUNTBATTEN: Somewhere high.

NEAVE: The dead are nothing. You'll get used to it, Sir.

Scene Five

Cliff top.
The OLD MAN, *with a wave of his stick.*

OLD MAN: The scene changes. Skim sideways across the Irish Sea and the face of our land.

Tyneside.

A moor.

A cliff.

I am Albion Yule, Jean's grandfather. I am very old. And extremely difficult.

The stick shoots out, pointing at someone in the wings.

You! Stagehand! Stop smoking! Don't you know smoking puts scum on your vital fluid?

I know the Bible backwards, and I disagree with every other word. I have been thrown out of more political meetings and church services than you have had fish suppers.

I keep my eyes open.

This scene in the North-East of England is dedicated to ten children and one old man – burnt to death in housing estates in Sunderland – between February 7th and March 15th. 1980.

Because their houses were lit by candles.

Because the electricity was cut off.

Because the bills raised by the Government could not be paid.

By an old man and unemployed parents.

Do we need human torches to light our way?

JEAN *comes on, the baby asleep on her back in a sling.*

JEAN: Grandad. Grandad.
Forgot what it was like out here. Wind like a brick. For crying out, loud, Grandpa!

They lean against the wind.

OLD MAN: Harlot!

Run to London!

Every face in that town – a mark of weakness, a mark of woe.

JEAN: But I'm come back.

OLD MAN: Rat! Failure! Kiss me!

He embraces her and jumps back, shocked.

The child is on your back! Should have the sky to look at, not a neck – thick with urban grime. Ha!

Come child. Let us sit upon the ground and tell each other statistics of decay in That Woman's England.

He plomps down on the floor.

JEAN: You live alone too much, Grandpa.

OLD MAN: Don't stand like a scarecrow on the skyline. Over the dying towns.

See that blur, far inland? Consett. A town under a death warrant. Steel town. 'Make a profit for us, your jobs will be saved' – said the British Steel Corporation. The workers made them a profit. Half a million pounds sterling in the first months of That Woman's Government. And phut! Closed. But who weeps? It's a long way from London.

What do you want?

JEAN sits down.

JEAN: I hitched. To ask you a question.

The OLD MAN, pleased.

OLD MAN: Ah! Dialectical!

He pumps the stick backwards and forwards.

JEAN: No, not really. Just life and death.

OLD MAN: Ah! Moral!

JEAN: Here it is. Here's the question. If things are as bad as you say, why don't I kill my baby?

She gestures at the baby.

Things are as bad as you say. So why don't I?

OLD MAN: Ha! I am an old man, but I can dance and sing.

JEAN: What does that mean?

OLD MAN: Fry the little thing alive. For supper. Slit up in rashers. I myself do not eat meat. Ha!

JEAN: You're not taking me seriously.

OLD MAN: Why should I? You don't. Lunatic despair, is it?

JEAN: Just a bit of suffering. Single parent family, sitting here. No job. In the world – know what I mean, Old Man?

OLD MAN: Hard times.

JEAN: I've heard them in the pubs. Men of your age. 'Hard times again, thirties again, old friends'.

OLD MAN: It's not. It's hard times forever.

He waves the stick.

So you're a steel man? Work in textiles. So you're in textiles? Sorry, we're moving to Germany. Sorry, unemployment in Germany. Be a real man. Get on the dole.

JEAN: Shut up, Grandad. I just want a bit of peace, right? Look.

She points the other way.

All my life, by the coast. Ruined castles by the sea. Saxon. Norman. Tudor. One by one – a chain of stone, down the coast.

He forces her by the shoulders to look back.

OLD MAN: You can't come up here to escape. Now there's a new chain. Ruined towns. Consett. Spennymore. Crook.

And – a rust in the chain. On the estates – one man in three out of work. A silence coming. A cold. An ice age, moving south.

JEAN: You've got a funny way of cheering me up.

The OLD MAN, with a very deep voice.

OLD MAN: Why do you think Christ descended into Hell? For a long weekend?

And when – was Christian – in *The Pilgrim's Progress*, most a hero?

JEAN (*aside*): Oh God. (*To the* OLD MAN:) When he did in Giant Despair, Grandad.

OLD MAN: Right!

He struggles up and stands, leaning on his stick.

I have, of late, wherefore I know not, come to see myself as a political party of one. At my last Annual Conference, I decided on a recruiting drive. Up!

JEAN: Oh God Grandad, no –

OLD MAN: My programme. One. A new Jerusalem. Two. Destroy That Woman.

A short silence.

JEAN: Yes?

OLD MAN: That's it.

JEAN: Oh.

OLD MAN: Has it been drinking orange juice? Are there aerated milk products in that child's diet? No? Then it will live. I have a toy for her.

He produces a ludicrously large conjurer's white rabbit from nowhere.

We'll rest you both. Then, this Political Party of three will go to London. Your friends are scattered. Your husband a reprobate. I will reunite us all. Human cell on cell. If I die, my ghost. If exorcised, the ghost of my stick.

He waves the stick in the air, crashes it down.

JEAN (*aside*): That's what I like about Grandad. He's a loony, but he thinks ahead.

Scene Six

NEAVE *wanders on.*

NEAVE: Loony? Loony? Did someone say loony?

Ladies and gentlemen, Sir Keith Joseph meets The Alien.

KEITH *shoots up onto the stage on a trap. He is holding a mirror. He looks at it and screams.*

NEAVE *goes off.*

KEITH: Arrgh! My face! My face!

Suddenly calm.

No it's all right it's my face.

He screams.

Arrgh! There's a tube going down my throat! It's sucking me inside out. Something strange. Like a reptile. Scaly, obscene, sterile. It's called –

He contorts. A voice from his bowels.

Mon-et-tar-ism.

He collapses and thrashes about on the floor, clutching his chest. Which bursts. PROFESSOR MILTON FRIEDMAN *shoots out.*

FRIEDMAN: Let the state play second fiddle to private enterprise. Life is a hoe-down.

KEITH: W-w-w-what are you, you unholy thing?

FRIEDMAN: Professor Milton Friedman.

KEITH *kneeling.*

KEITH: W-w-w-what must I do to be saved?

FRIEDMAN: Stop printing money on this planet.

KEITH: At last! A higher intelligence on Earth.

FRIEDMAN: You gotta let the rich get rich. Else the rich won't be rich.

KEITH: Oh, what is your message for mankind?

FRIEDMAN: Life is just a bite of cherry pie. If your teeth fall out, you can suck y'way to freedom. Ain't no one else gonna do it for you.

KEITH: I see!

FRIEDMAN: If I were born a coolie in downtown Hong Kong.

KEITH: Yes?

FRIEDMAN: Working in a sweat shop.

KEITH: Yes?

FRIEDMAN: More fool me. Hee haw ha!

The DUMMY *slaps its thigh.*

KEITH: They see things so clearly in America.

The DUMMY's *face close to* KEITH's. KEITH *mesmerised.*

FRIEDMAN: Now you're going to go through some pain, Bud.

KEITH: Pain?

FRIEDMAN: There is no short cut to economic recovery. Only one big cut.

KEITH: Cut?

FRIEDMAN: Like most of your country north of Euston Station.

KEITH: But Milton – people are living there. Or so I'm told.

FRIEDMAN: The Lord Jesus saw a barren fig tree, and cursed it, and it withered.

KEITH: But the future of Britain is glued to my hands.

KEITH *weeps.*

FRIEDMAN: Jiminy Cricket, don't despair. I don't, I smile all the time. 'Cos I know the answers. You got a steel industry?

KEITH: Oh no.

FRIEDMAN: You got cotton?

KEITH: Lancashire, falling to bits. Or so I'm told.

FRIEDMAN: You got English cars?

KEITH: British Leyland. Poor Michael Edwards. A bunny rabbit with blood in his mouth.

FRIEDMAN: No problem! Your cars and your cotton and your steel plated teapots – and your people, above all your people – don't make money – so – close 'em down.

KEITH: So clear. So –

A gesture.

Stupid it's almost obvious. So –

A gesture.

Brutal it's almost kind.

The DUMMY *leaps up onto* KEITH's *shoulder.*

FRIEDMAN: Be a crusade, Keith. Be an old world knight in shining armour. And a gas mask. Hee haw ha!

KEITH, *holding the dummy on his shoulder.*

KEITH (*aside*): Monetarism. Something simple. Faceless, flashing in the sunlight. Numbers, rows of figures, bland. I could have peace of mind. Yet!

The finger shoots up.

What haunts me is – if a Minister of Industry goes mad – and deaf – he will poison the industrial soil. Monstrous children with holes for faces – will crawl out of the badlands. And –

Arrgh! I'm frightening myself. The vein in my head, it'll burst. And Milton, I still can't sleep!

FRIEDMAN: Who needs sleep when they got power?

MARGARET *comes on.*

MARGARET: Keith. I've come to tell you how I'm going to run my Government.

KEITH, *stuffing the* DUMMY *up his jacket.*

KEITH: Oh God.

MARGARET: Now, there will be a little group of friends like you, who will decide everything in advance. I will just write down the agendas for the Cabinet and no one will have a vote. And I will give people the impression they are being browbeaten all the time. And they'll go away with the impression they've been humiliated. No one will need to know what's going on, because I will be going on. It's so good for democracy, for me to be elected.

Keith, what's wrong with your garden, dear?

KEITH *now looks like Richard III. He walks to her.*

KEITH: I've cut its development grant! Let things grow on their own.

MARGARET: What *are* those flowers?

KEITH: Dead men's fingers.

MARGARET, *straightening* KEITH's *clothes.*

MARGARET: Don't neglect yourself, use a pinny. I need you. Kiss?

She offers a cheek.

KEITH (*aside*): Oh, if only she knew the sordid side of my soul.

He kisses her cheek, awkwardly.

MARGARET: There are men, fat men –

KEITH: We must all eat less –

MARGARET: In my Cabinet, who think they are going to run the country through me. Because I am a woman.

KEITH: Flesh, flesh –

MARGARET: I am going to make a meal of them. When they come into the room, I will be standing. Or sometimes sitting. Or sometimes standing. Or sitting. I will withdraw my love.

KEITH: Fear, fear –

MARGARET: Shall we have tea? (*Steely.*) You invited me round for tea, Keith.

KEITH: Tea?

Mad.

There's water in the bathroom!

MARGARET: I have made one big mistake so far. I've not cut enough in my budget.

KEITH: Not your fault Margaret!

MARGARET: I know. Dear Geoffrey, even he is a little too – portly. You see Keith, we must chip and chip away, until there is a great, big, irreparable hole.

KEITH: A hole? Where?

MARGARET: Yes, be my feed Keith. A hole in the British way of life. Why should we love our neighbours? Why should I turn the other cheek? This is my best side. So. So. So. So.

A short silence.

I've run out of ideas, Keith.

KEITH (*aside*): My chance to spray her with my IQ!

(*To* MARGARET:) We all crawled out of the slime!

MARGARET, *head on one side.*

MARGARET: I see.

KEITH: The point about the Good Samaritan is he was very, very rich!

MARGARET: I'll make a note of that, mentally.

She blinks.

KEITH: It's just because of other people's envy that one does not drive one's Rolls Royce through the slums of Naples!

MARGARET: What you're telling me, Keith, is that poor people deserve to be poor.

KEITH: Absolutely! That's it!

MARGARET, *with an owlish smile, touching* KEITH's *arm.*

MARGARET: Keith, I've known that since I was a girl in Grantham.

KEITH: I had a nightmare, just before you came. All the policies of your Government going wrong. Not worth the pain of a Britain like ash. The north a poisoned desert. The south, a few good people and their gardens, cordoned off. The social fabric broken. And –

A short silence.

Communism, coming like a beast.

But now you're here, I'm all right.

MARGARET: That's because I believe in firm government, dear.

KEITH: And I *do* believe in human nature. Red in tooth and claw. Why stop human evolution with a Welfare State? Let the weak be the grass the strong walk upon. That's how God made the world, why should we interfere?

MARGARET: Can I use your sunlamp while we have tea? I want to look my best for the Party Conference.

They are going off, KEITH *weeping and carrying her shopping.*

KEITH: I do love the cruel world.

MARGARET: Have you got a boil on your back, Keith?

Scene Seven

Blackpool Beach.
MARGARET THATCHER*'s face in fairy-*
lights at the back.
The sound of the sea crashing on the beach
– then cut off.
NEAVE *shoots up onto the stage on the*
trap.

NEAVE: Blackpool Beach. Margaret's
New Britain.

He plays a few bars of 'I do like to be
beside the seaside' on a mouth organ
strapped to a severed arm. He bows and
goes off.

PIPKIN (*aside*): It's me. The renegade. At
the Tory Party Conference, Blackpool,
October 1979.

I've joined. On the way up. Four star
hotel. Delegations. Wife-swapping.
Funny voices. Drinking like frogs.

They all know each other. Now they
know me.

Outside the hotel – Right to Work
marchers, thalidomide boy playing a
bugle with his hands out of his shoulders.
In here – Michael Heseltine. Style.

A MAN comes on, circling in wonder. He
is George Formby-ish.

(*To the* MAN) Who are you? Are you a
man of power?

MAN (*with pride*): Conservative Trade
Unionist. What d'you think o' that?

PIPKIN: I don't believe in Trade Unions.

MAN (*crestfallen*): Oh.

Look. Jim Prior said his door's open to
me. Anytime I wanted.

PIPKIN: Yeah?

MAN: What d'you think o' that?

PIPKIN: Class traitor in't you. Like me.

MAN: No no! I've just found my place. Eee
see this?

He touches his throat.

It's me celluloid dicky. Me father wore
this 'day General Strike broke out.

A large MAN hurries across the stage,
surrounded by PHOTOGRAPHERS.
He stops, takes off sunglasses, grimaces,
puts sunglasses back on. Flash bulbs pop.
They go off.

Oh look! There's Willie Whitelaw! What
a big man. I'll just follow in his wake. My
father was so pitifully misled.

CONSERVATIVE TRADE
UNIONIST *goes off.*

PIPKIN: Poor sod. (*Aside.*) Oh I could wet
myself! If they catch my eye they'll find it
steady and true. I want to be a Tory
Candidate. Shout about freedom and
responsibility and putting the boot in! Be
on 'Any Questions' and get cheered!

When you're a Delegate at the Tory
Conference, you got to keep your
Y-fronts straight. Maybe Margaret will
pass me. Slip on a banana skin and fall
into my arms. And give me a car with a
phone in it.

He cups his hands and sniffs his breath.
Smiles.
A White Rhodesian THUG, *an upper-*
class DEGENERATE *and a blousy*
WOMAN *come on.*

DEGENERATE: Margaret is on our side.
She just has to choose her words. What
did she say? Swamped by aliens.

WOMAN: I wonder why Enoch's gone so
far to the left?

PIPKIN (*aside*): Oh look. Fascists! No no.
They're just strange. New Tory Party. I
love it. It's tasty.

THUG (*aside*): I am a White ex-Rhodesian
thug. Making a new life in Epsom.

WOMAN (*aside*): I am in the Monday
Club. I like the stink of hate.

DEGENERATE (*aside*): I am an upper-
class degenerate. I have a receding
forehead, long dirty finger-nails, money
and power. I am also a real person seen at
the Tory Conference by our authors. I
am probably waiting for you outside.

THUG: I've poisoned wells. I've killed my
man. It's not true that Hitler killed the
Jews. But if I had my way I'd do the same.

With the immigrants in this country. Of
mine.

PIPKIN (*aside*): The Socialists hope they've
got the National Front licked. Actually
they've all just joined the Tory Party.

THUG: If I had my way I'd bomb Ireland with yellow gas.

WOMAN: Knee-cap the survivors.

DEGENERATE: People don't know the meaning of fear. Yet.

PIPKIN: It's all true. Everything I've been told about the Tories. It's horrible, horrible. And it's great.

Scene Eight

Blackpool beach, night.
The CONSERVATIVE TRADE UNIONIST *comes on drunk, with a bottle.*

DRUNK: Good old Margaret! Good old Margaret! Where are you, come on Maggie, save Britain!

He staggers off.

The OLD MAN *comes on.*

OLD MAN: Blackpool beach. Two a.m. Night of the Young Conservative's Ball.

He raises his stick to the sky.

The Dog Star conspicuous.

He lowers the stick.

I will now thunder across these footlights my utter contempt.

He takes a deep breath.

What is this species? What is this life-form? What trick of Social-Darwinism has made these loathesome things crawl up the people's beach?

Waving his stick.

How can I, who believe in the Brother-hood of Man, find myself, faced by this lot, consumed with thoughts of genocide?

He lowers the stick.

I leave my granddaughter and the child on the outskirts. I descend into this pit to save the reprobate husband.

PIPKIN *comes on with* GLORIA. *She is masked. She seems to be 'County', she wears a ball gown with a man's coat-and-tails round her shoulders.*

GLORIA: Are you really working-class, Pipkin?

OLD MAN (*aside*): The renegade! Found!

He withdraws to listen.

PIPKIN: Yes, aren't you living dangerously, 'Doll'. Your Dad loaded, is he?

GLORIA: Gosh – and are you really a Tory?

PIPKIN: Course I joined. Party of indi-vidualists, in't it? Where any man can rise. As I could to you, Doll. Hangabout – who's coat is that?

GLORIA: His name is Rodney Sangster and he's a bore. He talks about politics all the time.

PIPKIN: And you're, er, really from the shires? Hunting? Stirrup cup and that?

GLORIA: Wolverhampton actually. There isn't a hunt in Wolverhampton.

PIPKIN: I don't know. Get the dogs on the coons –

GLORIA: I say, that's bad form.

PIPKIN: Tories in't we? All got Enoch tattooed – inside our lip.

He rubs his lower lip.

GLORIA: We mustn't talk about Mr Powell. Though of course we all know –

PIPKIN: What?

GLORIA: You know.

PIPKIN: What?

She fingers the coat.

GLORIA: I think Rodney –

PIPKIN: We're Tories, we're racists.

GLORIA: Don't put it like that. Gosh you're gauche. What's that star?

PIPKIN: Our lucky star.

They embrace.

OLD MAN: Stop! Babylon!

GLORIA: Godfathers –

OLD MAN: That man is married with a child!

He crashes the stick down between PIPKIN and GLORIA, who jump away just in time.

PIPKIN: Who are you? What are y'doing?

OLD MAN: Shall I kill you now, or will history do the job?

GLORIA: Police!

The OLD MAN pushes her away with the stick.

OLD MAN: I have heard of your paintings well enough. To a nunnery, go. (*Aside.*) Hamlet.

GLORIA, *backing away.*

GLORIA: Rodney. Oh Rodney, where are you – it's the Right To Work Campaign –

She runs off.

The OLD MAN *turns on* PIPKIN, *who raises a warning finger.*

PIPKIN: Steady –

OLD MAN: Return at once! If not to your family, then to your roots!

PIPKIN: You're the grandfather –

OLD MAN: Shall I beat you into the sea?

PIPKIN: Could and all, couldn't you. Mad family. Like wandering Jews.

The OLD MAN *raises the stick.*

OLD MAN: You insult yourself!

PIPKIN: Everything you love is dying. Margaret Thatcher won't flinch, even from a new World War. I'm glad, 'cos I'm British. Aren't you?

OLD MAN: You Judas goat! That woman marked you out! With your kind they divide and rule.

PIPKIN: It's the new age of self-interest come at last. The rest of you can rot. I'm a class traitor, one hundred per cent. I'm a Tory. I got dignity – 'cos I'm all out for me.

The OLD MAN *lowers the stick. He is suddenly weary.*

OLD MAN: Take it – you have been beaten – into the sea.

The OLD MAN *turns away.*

PIPKIN: Loon!

PIPKIN *kicks sand. He looks up.*

Lucky star.

A SECURITY MAN *comes on. He wears an evening suit and carries a bunch of flowers in cellophane. He pushes* PIPKIN *away, poking him in the chest.*

SECURITY MAN: All right.

PIPKIN: Eh –

SECURITY MAN: All right.

PIPKIN: Eh. Beach.

SECURITY MAN: All right.

PIPKIN *looks over the* SECURITY MAN's *shoulder.*

PIPKIN: It's her! It's Margaret!

SECURITY MAN: All right.

PIPKIN: I want to talk to her. I want to tell her. I got so much to explain to her.

SECURITY MAN: All right.

PIPKIN is off the stage. The SECURITY MAN turns back. MARGARET THATCHER comes on dressed in a ball gown. More SECURITY MEN come on in evening dress, all carrying bunches of flowers in cellophane. They are watchful around her.

MARGARET: So pretty, the lights. For the children. I'm sorry, did you all want to dance on at the ball?

SECURITY MEN: No Ma'am, no Ma'am, thank you, Ma'am.

MARGARET: I only dance once at the YC Ball. You know, Lord Thorneycroft tells me you can see Ireland from the top of the Blackpool Tower.

The DRUNK comes on with a bottle.

DRUNK (*shouts*): Come on Maggie! Save Britain!

He throws the bottle.
The SECURITY GUARDS electrify – suddenly they all have guns in their hands, in a circle around her.

MARGARET (*aside*): You have been waiting for a few words of comfort from me.

Here they are.

The woman's place is in the kitchen. You men – make money, be men. All of you – stop snivelling. I am not afraid of unemployment. I am not afraid of the unemployed. I am not afraid of the nuclear war with Russia. Thank you for electing me. There.

ACT TWO

Scene One

Sunlight filtering through slatted blinds. SIR KEITH JOSEPH lies on the floor, in chains. The GHOST OF AIREY NEAVE stands to one side.

NEAVE: Odd, the clarity you get when you're dead.

I look at Margaret Thatcher's Britain now, like a little unseen satellite.

One year gone and high summer come. Ten companies collapsing every day. Queues of directors at the bank with begging bowls. The CBI says 'you promised us a phoenix but all we can see are ashes.'

Cabinet Ministers pull on their socks at dawn and ask – who's for the chop? What's going wrong? Has the crisis come?

Ladies and Gentlemen. Twenty-four hours of government life. In a little dark room in Chelsea, Sir Keith Joseph finds government hard going.

KEITH: Oh the sweet earth. Good and bad, the ripples on the sea of human faces. The talented and the untalented – the talent-free. The swimming and the drowned. You all hate me. You do, you do. Therefore – I must be right. I am so without honour in my own country that I must be a prophet. I must have a vision! If I could cut myself I'd see it.

He whips himself and screams.

No, no, back to work. We must go forward. Back to the nineteenth century! The capitalist was free then. And the horror of the slums was a great tourist attraction. The steam engine! The cholera! Oh happy time, come back!

He whips himself, screams.

A FREE SOCIETY. A land with plenty of ladders. And a good cheap safety net. A land in which people decide, aspire, succeed, fail and despair.

He writes on the floor.

It's come to me! There is no working class. Only the wicked, the maimed and the thick.

Enter NORMAN ST JOHN STEVAS,
nervously.

NORMA: H – hullo Keith.

KEITH: Who are you?

NORMAN: I'm Norman St John Stevas.
(*Aside*.) Oh happy court of Margaret
where so many geniuses glitter.

KEITH: Have you brought the knife?

NORMAN: Knife?

KEITH: To kill me!

NORMAN: I'm Minister of the Arts, Keith.

KEITH: Arrrgh! The last of the big
spenders!

KEITH *attacks* NORMAN.

NORMAN: Don't damage my style. Style is
all when you have to lead the House of
Commons.

I'm Margaret's shop-window.

KEITH *stops the attack and slinks away*.

KEITH: Oh St John, St John, sing to me.

NORMAN: I can't. I'm a little tense.
Margaret's sent me with a message.

KEITH: What's happened? Did I miss the
Third World War?

NORMAN: No. Really bad news.
'Emergency cabinet meeting. The wets
want a U-turn. Tonight.'

KEITH: But I've nearly made England
great!

We must not run away. Every Tory
Government since the war has run away.
First sight of the rats, the packs of people,
the unions.

Ted Heath – compromised, cowered and
was crushed. And I, even I did not resign.
I am so ashamed.

Don't you agree?

NORMAN: Yes! Yes!

(*He crosses himself*.) Oh God forgive me,
I'm too wet to be the wet I want to be.

KEITH: Oh St John , St John! What can we
do, we morbid right-wing thinkers?

NORMAN: More money for the Arts?

KEITH *shoves him away and cracks the
whip at his feet*. NORMAN *hops with a*

squeak. KEITH *shoots a finger up*.

KEITH: Block up their rat-holes with anit-
union laws, let them die quietly, in little
clusters, in the wall. Steel strikers and
their families – ssh, listen. Not a
scratching in the wall.

(*The latest figures, in a torrent*.) In two
weeks: Birmingham, Sheffield, Glasgow,
Oldham, Northampton, Liverpool, 600,
850, 500, 850, 800, 550 – 5,365 jobs lost in
just fourteen days.

It's working! So many people free!
Everyone knows a monetary policy
means 3,000,000 unemployed.

NORMAN: My God! That's 7,500 full
houses at the Theatre Royal, Stratford
East. Pity they won't have any money to
get in.

KEITH: We need an iron man.

NORMAN: Haven't we got one? Chap
called Jim Prior.

KEITH: AAAAAAAAAAARGH!

Scene Two

A loud noise of farm animals. It stops.
JIM PRIOR *comes on. He is dis-*
embowelling a dead calf, blood up to his
elbows. Two bushes are pushed on. The
GHOST OF AIREY NEAVE *stands to*
one side.

NEAVE (*aside*): Eleven a.m., Sunday. By a
moated farmhouse in Suffolk, decent Jim
Prior, who wouldn't be caught dead
talking to himself, talks to himself.

JIM: U-turn? Up-turn? U-turn – down-
turn. Common sense. Pursue steady
path, good boring policies – but best
Conservative policies are – boring.

NEAVE: Jim Prior is sometime director of
Aston Boats, Boggis Engineering,
Hazleworth Properties, Lambert and Son
Tobacco Blenders, Lynwood Caravans,
Norwich Union Insurance, and Avon
Cosmetics.

A WOMAN'S VOICE (*off*): Telephone,
darling.

JIM: I'll take it in the wheelbarrow.

A GARDENER comes on with a
wheelbarrow. JIM lifts a telephone
receiver from it.

What? No I can't talk to Ted. Bush?
What Bush? Oh dear.

He puts the telephone back and sidles up to
a bush.

I wish you wouldn't Ted. Don't go down
so low, Ted.

The bush rustles.

Anyway, I can't talk to you. I'll be
punished. They're very cruel.

The GARDENER stares.

They call us wets. They call me a softy.
Bed of nails, bed of knives. I still can't
understand what makes Keith tick – and
Margaret, she goes alone with it!

WILLIE (*off*): It's all right Jane – I'll bowl
on out to him.

WILLIE WHITELAW *comes on. He is*
with a BLIND POLICEMAN, *who holds*
a white cane. NEAVE *pointing at his*
head.

NEAVE: William Whitelaw, Home
Secretary, golfer and farmer. A cow man.

Ran against Margaret Thatcher for the
Leadership. Got himself photographed at
a sink wearing a pinny. Lost. Got himself
photographed kissing Margaret Thatcher
in the street.

JIM: I'm not talking to you, Willie. You're a
traitor to Ted.

WILLIE: No I'm not. I'm everyone's
friend.

BLIND POLICEMAN *discovers the*
GARDENER.

POLICEMAN: When did you enter this
country?

The GARDENER *suffers.*

JIM: What do you want Willie? Come to put
the frighteners on me, have you?

WILLIE: Emergency Cabinet meeting.
About you. She thinks you're talking to
Ted.

PRIOR *backing towards bush.*

JIM: I won't be warned off. I've pulled the
horns off heiffers. I can come back to my
bloody farm.

WILLIE: We can all go back to our bloody
farms.

JIM: Government under Ted used to be
fun. 'Course it all ended in in disaster, but
being chums together was good. You
loved it, Willie. You were Ted's bright-
eyed baby boy.

WILLIE: I'm loyal. A leader's got to have
something to lead. Here I am. Look Jim,
dog to man, I mean man to man –
statesman to statesman – just bash the
unions and I'll lock 'em up for you.

JIM: We need working people you know.
Who's going to do the work? I mean – I've
employed men. Cycle of the land, cycle of
Labour. Reasonable pay deals agreed
with the TUC – early Spring. Autumn-
sileage out of the clamps, eyes down for
another pay round. Everyone more or
less getting along. I mean what's
Margaret up to, in London surrounded by
cranks? Cardigans. Yankee economists.
Keith, since he went potty –

WILLIE: Oh, I know I've got a second-rate
brain –

JIM: I'm in despair – or would be, if I
weren't so cheerful.

WILLIE: She does need you, you know.

He puts his arm round JIM.

WILLIE: That's why she's so bitchy about you. You're the acceptable face of Conservatism. Come on. Back to town – face the music.

WILLIE *strides off.*

JIM (*to bush*): I'm sorry, Ted. It really is like you're dead, Ted. But I'm here alive.

POLICEMAN: Is your passport lodged with the Home Office?

JIM: I'm not black, I'm a Cabinet Minister.

POLICEMAN: Sorry, sir.

JIM *looks at his watch.*

JIM: Gulp. High noon.

JIM *and the* POLICEMAN *go off.*

Scene Three

Evening. On the road. A front cloth, leaving a shallow stage.

On the cloth the Fiat care advertisement – 'HANDBUILT BY ROBOTS'. Then the roar of fast travelling cars for a moment – then cut off. It gets darker through the scene.

The OLD MAN *and* JEAN *are hitching.* JEAN *has the baby on her back in a sling, and a bit of cardboard, chalked on it 'LONDON'.*

JEAN: Hitching to London. Sunday.

OLD MAN: Stop!

JEAN: I'm carrying a crazy old man on my head. Give it up Jean. (*To the* OLD MAN.) Don't stand in the road.

OLD MAN: You hyenas! I'll wrench you from your cars!

JEAN: You're supposed to look harmless Grandad, when you're hitching.

OLD MAN: I will appropriate a vehicle. This is Party business –

JEAN: Party of two and a kid –

OLD MAN: How can I circumlocute the country, building revolutionary cells, at the whim of a travelling meatpie salesman?

JEAN: You and Tina hide behind the bill-board. I'll wiggle my backside at a driver.

OLD MAN: Sexual exploitation of the democratic right to travel? Babylon!

JEAN: Your foot's worse.

OLD MAN: The foot is lost to me. Let it bleed.

He stumbles.

You may, under the circumstances, expose your thigh.

JEAN: I'll just smile.

She adopts a frozen smile.

OLD MAN (*aside*): A journey of a thousand miles, through That Woman's Britain, on a bleeding foot.

North-East, South-West. North-West, West. The dereliction. The British People. Groups huddled in the corners of pubs, of clubs, of streets, of their own homes.

Go into the town. The shops. Girls by tills waiting for something to do. The winter sales going on for weeks.

Big men, seen through their living-room windows, watching television in the afternoon.

At the docksides – men stripped of the right to work. Eyeing me.

Our country looks the way it always looked. But look again – you see the planet Mars.

JEAN (*aside*): The de-industrialisation of Britain.

OLD MAN: I'm cold.

JEAN (*aside*): The ice-age.

OLD MAN: Night coming down.

The sound of a car drawing up.

Scene Four

10 Downing Street. Two henchmen, BIFFO *and* NOTT.

BIFFO (*aside*): The White Drawing Room, Downing Street. Two a.m.

A clock chimes.

NOTT (*aside*): The witching hour.

They point at each other's heads.

BIFFO: John Nott.

NOTT: John Biffen. He goes on TV to tell you we're going to make things really horrible for you.

BIFFO: He goes on TV to tell you how he won't tell you Dennis Thatcher's company is starving the South African blacks.

NOTT: Urtcha.

BIFFO: Urtcha.

GEOFFREY HOWE *wheels in* MARGARET. *He has a lighter-than-air balloon tied to the quiff in his hair. The balloon has a £ sign on it.* MARGARET *sits in a large, padded sitting room chair – cosy and comfy, white with floral pattern, chintz skirts, high back, antimacassar. Behind her chair there is placed a bird-cage on a pole. The cage has live rats in it.*

MARGARET (*aside*): The business of good Tory government. In a time of crisis.

GEOFFREY (*looking up at his balloon*): Sorry about the pound, Margaret.

MARGARET: That's all right, Geoffrey. Every Chancellor of the Exchequer has something out of control. Anyway, a good politician doesn't admit there's a crisis. You just get blood on your knitting needles.

Begin!

NOTT *and* BIFFO, BIFFO *with a chainsaw, rush on a* BACKBENCHER, *who is blindfolded. He wears no tie but a noose round his neck and is barefoot. A big blue rosette is on his breast.*

BACKBENCHER: No! No! Not Nott and Biffo Biffen!

They rip the blindfold off. He sees the chainsaw.

Oh God help me. The Treasury.

MARGARET: Who have you got there? Jim Prior?

BIFFO: No. Julian. A dirty little traitor –

NOTT: One of many –

BIFFO: Wrote an article in the *Observer* –

NOTT: Criticising you –

NOTT offers newspapers. MARGARET ignores them, GEOFFREY grabs one and tears it up, not reading it.

GEOFFREY: 'Cabinet rift in the open'!

NOTT: 'Backbencher says Jim Prior a reasonable man'!

NOTT tears up a newspaper. Eats it.

MARGARET (*to the* BACKBENCHER): Hello Julian. How's your dental trouble?

BACKBENCHER (*terrified*): M-M-M-M-M-M-M-M-M My upper plate –

NOTT: You're lucky we're being so nice to you Julian –

BIFFO: Just smashing your teeth and breaking your fingers –

NOTT: Under Ted you'd have been up in the whips' office –

BIFFO: Having your balls swopped over. Sorry Margaret.

MARGARET: Think of me as a man over this one.

GEOFFREY: Get it into your head. You're just there to boo Dennis Healey on the radio. (*He twitches.*) That pig.

NOTT: Not piss on your leader's shoes!

MARGARET: Is there anything wrong at home?

BACKBENCHER: I'm a Conservative MP with a majority of 24,000 and they don't understand why prices are going mad –

MARGARET: They voted for us, dear. Go and tell them, in a democracy they vote once and go to sleep for five years.

She offers a cheek.

What a wonderful film *The Angry Silence* was.

Kiss.

The BACKBENCHER *pecks at her cheek.*

Take him away.

BIFFO *and* NOTT, *dragging him off.*

BACKBENCHER: Oh why did you put up VAT!

He's gone. GEOFFREY *and* MARGARET *alone.*

MARGARET: Are there any more of them?

GEOFFREY: Lots. Hanging on coatpegs in the hall.

Sawings and screams off.

MARGARET: Funny how Jim Prior is the only effective opposition in this country. Why are the Labour Party so quiet? Nobody's giving them anything, are they?

GEOFFREY: They're all neurotic about Dennis Healey. A man with eyebrows that big must be trying to hide something.

He twitches.

MARGARET: Not tired are you, Geoffrey? It's only two o'clock in the morning.

GEOFFREY: No no no. It's just that running a Government at night gives you funny bowels.

MARGARET: I've always made do on six hours at the most. Two at the moment. Have an aspro.

She offers him an aspro only to withdraw it. She goes into a reverie.

They think I'm weak because I'm a woman. They think I'll cry on TV, my voice will go funny and hysterical.

They think I'm brittle, think I'll crack.

Men are always afraid of strong women. Like poor Joan of Arc.

I like my hair well shaped, I like my make-up hard. I sit here bright, while men smell and argue and feel dirty around me. It works.

GEOFFREY: Women are so much more logical than men.

MARGARET: No, Geoffrey. I am so much more logical than you. I'm glad there are even fewer women in Parliament now. I shine the more. Who shall I shine on now? Norman!

NORMAN *enters. He wears an opera cloak.*

NORMAN: Ah Margaretta. Kiss.

He blows gold dust from his palm.

MARGARET: Norman, you're so flashy –

GEOFFREY (*sotto*): Bread and circuses.

MARGARET: Not like Airey. And where have you been?

NORMAN: To see the Peking Opera.

MARGARET: Where are they on?

NORMAN: Peking.

MARGARET: So witty.

GEOFFREY: There's dead butterflies on your collar.

NORMAN: They follow me about. Where's Keith?

GEOFFREY: Disappeared. But I've stuffed my bum in front of the fire.

NORMAN: Oh, why is government so sordid, so animal? All the lies we've told. I am Leader of the House of Commons, a mere corrupter of consciences. I'd like to see myself as the Tory Party's Hamlet – but I can't stand leaping about in people's graves.

MARGARET (*she laughs*): Norman, you're so sensitive, I like you. Now shut up.

GEOFFREY: What's the use of sensitivity? What's the use of democracy? People talk about right and wrong and they can't even bloody well add up. Trouble with me, my ego's not big enough.

NORMAN: Giving Jim Prior your job? Had the U-turn have we?

GEOFFREY: What?

NORMAN: That's what they're saying in Peking. (*To* MARGARET:) Are you sure it's the right policy, friendship with China? Opera was bloody awful.

A VIOLINIST *comes on, playing.*

VIOLINIST: Gentlemen and Ma'am. The Foreign Secretary of Great Britain, Lord Peter Carrington.

NORMAN: Oh these glamorous nights.

VIOLINIST *plays 'Jealousy'.* LORD PETER CARRINGTON *sweeps in in a fine suit and a solar top. He pays great attention to his cuffs. He glides to* MARGARET.

CARRINGTON: I've juist come from Fi-fi's. The place is alive with rumours of a U-turn.

MARGARET: Peter, I don't want you going to places like that. Kiss?

CARRINGTON *swoops and kisses.*

MARGARET: Oh Peter.

CARRINGTON: Margaret dear, shall we tango the night away like we did in Lusaka?

GEOFFREY: She's got the aspros out.

CARRINGTON: Oh God. Fatty Prior getting his tonight?

GEOFFREY: Yup.

CARRINGTON: Margaret dear, I know we ended up with a Marxist Government in Rhodesia –

MARGARET (*steely*): Yes. I never did quite understand that.

CARRINGTON: But we must have a foreign policy Margaret. Other than bombing Russia flat.

Flexing his hand; knuckles cracking.

And breaking the legs of Olympic athletes. Please. I want to be a great man. I'm not going down in the history books as the only British Foreign Secretary who ushered in a Government of Marxist Blacks!

MARGARET: Peter – what do you want to do – ?

CARRINGTON: Ireland.

The VIOLINIST *stops in mid-note. All glare with horror. A silence.*

MARGARET: Peter, I don't think you should go on.

CARRINGTON: We had a settlement in Rhodesia. Why not a settlement in Ireland –

MARGARET: No –

CARRINGTON: After 800 years.

MARGARET: No –

CARRINGTON: Think the unthinkable.

MARGARET: No –

CARRINGTON: I'm talking to you straight you bitch –

MARGARET, *with fury.*

MARGARET: Get me my flak jacket!

CARRINGTON: It's my last chance!

MARGARET (*at* NORMAN): In the bag behind my chair.

CARRINGTON: It's the only colony we've got left!

MARGARET, *struggling into the flak jacket.*

MARGARET: It's not a colony! Airey always said it was part of Britain. You can't play with people's lives.

CARRINGTON: Real Tories do play with people's lives.

MARGARET (*screams*): Aaaaaaargh!

A silence.

It's my Cuba.

A silence.

(*Screams.*) Aaaaaaargh!

A silence.

(*Screams.*) Aaaaaaargh!

A silence. All are dead still except the rats in the cage. Then MARGARET *calmly.*

Now that everyone's had their say, I'll have mine. Tell everyone they must try – To get – Their spelling better – In their Cabinet papers.

CARRINGTON (*low*): Yes Margaret –

NORMAN (*low*): Yes Margaret –

GEOFFREY (*low*): Yes Margaret –

CARRINGTON (*low*): Oh damn greatness, damn damn greatness.

BIFFO: Len Murray's on the phone. He's ringing from a callbox.

GEOFFREY: Who?

BIFFO: Say's he's from the TUC.

GEOFFREY: The what?

MARGARET: So many cranks ring us up at night. Tell him to go away. The night does strange things to people.

She stares into the distance.

On these nights in Downing Street, I do sometimes look out of the window and I fancy I see Airey. In the shadows, the other side of the street.

BIFFO: And Willie Whitelaw's here with Fatty Prior.

MARGARET: Oh good.

LORD PETER: Oh God.

GEOFFREY, *rubbing his hands.*

GEOFFREY (*to* NORMAN): Someone's going to leave this room tonight without his giblets.

MARGARET: Now no one's going to write on the walls. No one's going to pee in their trousers. And nobody is going to shout.

Mr Nott and Mr Biffin we're ready now.

BIFFO: The Cabinet is now in session.

ALL: Goody goody goody.

Everyone looks off stage. BIFFO *and* NOTT *come on following them* WILLIE WHITELAW, *and* JIM PRIOR *who wears an orange anorak. He carries a blood-stained sack. The* BLIND POLICEMAN *is in attendance and starts to patrol, fingering* GEOFFREY.

WILLIE: Sorry we're late, Margaret.

He slobbers kisses on her face.

Got stuck on the North Circular. Did a U-turn.

He sniggers.

JIM: Brought your meat for your deep freeze Margaret.

He hefts the meat onto the floor. CARRINGTON *grimaces.*

MARGARET: Thank you Jim. Willie, go and change your trousers.

WILLIE *looking down.*

WILLIE: S'all right, Margaret. I can take a bollocking, 'well as give it.

POLICEMAN (*to* GEOFFREY): Are you wearing a dress, sir?

WILLIE *shambles off stage.*

WILLIE: Officer! (*Aside.*) I used to run Ireland. Now I run immigrants out of the country. I like my work. Don't look me in the eye.

NORMAN: I think I'll get a lift to confession, in his little panda.

MARGARET: No. You'll stay and learn what Toryism is all about.

The BLIND POLICEMAN *follows* WILLIE *off.*

MARGARET: Well Jim. Aren't you ashamed of yourself?

JIM: Am I? What?

(*Aside.*) Keep fighting, Jim.

(*To* MARGARET:) No no no no no no I'm not, Margaret. See old girl, I'm not the oaf I take me for. I am the embod-i-a-ment of all the experienced Conservatives who think you'll ruin us all.

A silence.

Old girl.

A silence.

Let me blind you with science. My Employment Bill.

He takes out a large file and shakes it. A concertina of paper shoots across the stage.

Now, I'm tough. And this is tough.

On the unions.

Which is what you want me to be. Isn't it, Margaret?

He shoots through several yards of the concertina, then stabs at a passage.

Look at this, I'm going to repeal Schedule 11 of the Employment Protection Act.

CARRINGTON: Oh God. Why don't we just invade Iran and forget all our troubles.

JIM: Wage cutting. Legalise it.

CARRINGTON: I mean – why does everybody worry about money so much? I own half of Buckinghamshire and I don't worry about money.

MARGARET: Where's that nice bit about wage cutting, Jim?

JIM (*he unleashes a battery of magic tricks*): And another thing Margaret, when people want a union in their factory, I'm going to stop them going to ACAS. Advice, Conciliation, Arbitration, that's not tough, is it? Some employees are dis-puting, they'll have to fight it out on their own on the streets. We can send the *Daily Mail* round to take some violent snaps, put 'em in a bad light and there you are, Margaret – every day, Grunwicks and Grunwicks and Grun –

MARGARET: Jim.

JIM: What?

MARGARET: No one can understand the Employment Bill.

JIM: That's the point. If they can't understand it they can't fight it. That's why it's so tough.

MARGARET: How are you going to stop picketing?

BIFFO (*low*): The boot.

NOTT (*low*): Troops.

JIM: I'm going to take the right to picket away.

MARGARET: Reams and reams of reason James. Just make me one simple law to take away their privileges.

JIM: Their rights –

MARGARET: Privileges –

JIM: Oh. All right I will.

MARGARET: And – take away their funds. And, if they get difficult, turn them into criminals. Criminals. Now.

GEOFFREY: You fat bed-bug. I'm doing my bit. I tax the unemployed –

MARGARET: Yes Geoffrey, tell Jim what *you're* doing to make England pleasant.

GEOFFREY: Sick, injured, pregnant I'm doing 'em all.

MARGARET: Geoffrey pretends –

GEOFFREY: I pretend striker's families are on strike as well. And dock 'em twelve pounds a week. You can use a budget like a meat cleaver if you've got ideals.

MARGARET: Jim. What did I get power for?

JIM: Rule the country old girl –

MARGARET: No dear. Divide the country.

JIM: But that's not fun.

MARGARET: Only great adventures thrill

me, Jim. An irreversible change. People *will* learn, *will* take their medicine. Britain is my little shop. There will be no U-turn. If I go under, you all go under.

GEOFFREY: Oh my God.

JIM: Got to go slowly. Can't nobble 'em all in one go. See how this chunk goes down then we can have another look –

MARGARET: All or nothing.

NORMAN: Let them eat Wagner?

JIM: Softly softly with the big stick, or you'll have a General Strike!

NOTT *and* BIFFO *giggling and nudging each other, a schoolboy sing-song.*

BIFFO: Never never – Day of Action Day
NOTT: of Action – South Wales miners – yellow yellow –

NORMAN: Listen to the silence.

A silence.

I wonder what the *decent* people are dreaming tonight.

Shop keepers over their shops. Who despise they who beg for Social Security.

Young people with talent, who dream of a little business and voted for me instead of the National Front.

The little Englanders, in the little towns, who begin to laugh in their sleep, because the lights are on in Downing Street. And we are going – without any fuss at all – to smash organised Labour.

JIM: Oh you silly arses! You'll spoil it for us all. I know about men – years and years and years of deceiving the people of this country – years of experience with good old Ted –

BIFFO: That's not a pee in his trousers, that's a poop.

JIM: Godammit woman! You did a U-turn under Ted! You didn't resign!

GEOFFREY: That's it. Heard enough. Down with his trousers.

JIM: Oh no, don't be cruel –

GEOFFREY: Boot polish. Black balls.

NOTT *produces a tin and a big shoe brush.*

Political influence is very like a bank account. Yours is overdrawn, old man.

NOTT, BIFFO *and* GEOFFREY *down* JIM *onto the floor to de-bag him.*

NORMAN: Oh I hope I don't miss early mass.

JIM: Look all you chums – Public Expenditure in this country is the lowest in Europe. You must know what you're doing is mad.

NOTT: Wogs begin at Calais, Fatty.

BIFFO: Brighton.

JIM: I'll tell the *Guardian*! I'll go on TV and say Ted was better than you!

MARGARET: What is it, Jim, that all Tories have?

JIM (*miserably*): Oh, loyalty.

JIM *suffers.*

MARGARET: Do you know, Peter, there's an enterprising man in America who's got five Nobel-Prize-winners to donate their – manly juices. So bright girls can have their babies. That kind Mr Milton Friedman sent me some of his.

She produces a huge coca-cola bottle from her handbag, full of white liquid.

CHARRINGTON (*staring*): My God.

She opens it with her teeth. GEOFFREY *takes it.*

GEOFFREY: You've got no spunk, Jim. Open wide.

JIM: Urgh please.

GEOFFREY: Take your medicine.

JIM: Glug glug.

GEOFFREY (*aside*): The milk of monetarism.

CARRINGTON (*aside*): Why do I go along with these perverts and banditti? Robbing the poor to give to the stinking rich? Must be the romantic in me.

WILLIE *comes on with a towel and no trousers. The* BLIND POLICEMAN *carries a corpse.*

WILLIE: Margaret. They keep on finding corpses in police stations.

The BLIND POLICEMAN *drops the body and begins groping and clubbing it.* KEITH *comes on covered in eggs and*

tomatoes and carrying a placard – KEITH
YOU ARE MAD AND WE HATE
YOU.

KEITH: I bring you Good News! The poor
do not exist.

MARGARET: Thank you. It's only four
o'clock. Shall we make some cuts?

Scene Five

The shop at night. The projector is running a
film about the Tory cuts, without sound.
MILLY *sits on a rubber cushion.*

MILLY (*aside*): Milly again.

Thatcher!

Ooh – tonight she's got me in my
backside. All night I've been dug into my
Local Labour Party, doing my bit for
Tony Benn. I hope that guy is Father
Christmas – a lot of us are losing a lot of
stomach wall. If you're sat on a
committee trying to democratize Labour
what do you need? An iron bum. Tired.
All on my own. Arthur in hospital. He
nudged a policeman on the Blair Peach
Memorial march.

A crash.

ARTHUR (*off*): Help!

ARTHUR *walks through the movie*
screen. He wears an old mackintosh over
hospital pyjamas. He holds a drip feed up
in one hand.

I want a drink!

MILLY: Arthur – get back to hospital!

ARTHUR: They've closed it down.

When I'm lathered up I'll nip back and
arm the nurses with me Civil War pikes.

MILLY: Don't lower your arm! Your
blood'll run out.

ARTHUR (*aside*): If the Tories want to
fight the sick and dying let them do it in
the open.

MILLY: Oh Arthur –

ARTHUR: I've got my tactics clear. Mount
campaigns! Be termites! Crawl up their
legs and chew 'em away. I'm into issue
politics now.

MILLY: You do keep on changing your
politics, Arthur.

ARTHUR (*crestfallen*): Do I? Oh.

Happy again.

All right then, I'll rejoin the CP. (*Aside.*)
At least they got analysis and backbone.
We can't all just be sputtering candles.

MILLY: You got gin in that drip?

ARTHUR: The adrenalin of anger, my

love. My legs are about to go.

He collapses.

Told you.

Banging and dog-like howls off. PIPKIN *comes on through the screen. He wears a businessman's suit, torn, a wrecked white shirt and chewed blue ties. He drags a dead dog on a lead. He kicks the dead dog.*

PIPKIN (*aside*): I am the Thatcher Experiment. Proved wrong.

He kicks the dog.

Kill, Margaret. Kill, kill! (*Aside.*) I sussed it out. Set up a small business, breeding Alsation dogs. A big market – the South London middle class, scared to death of the burglaring poor, rampaging through their houses.

Mad.

But I can't pay the VAT!

MILLY: Pipkin, mate –

PIPKIN: It's all right Milly. I'm in hell. The bailiffs'll be in in two hours time. I'll have to drown my stock on Peckham Rye.

Kissing the dog.

Oh come on Maggie, save Britain.

MILLY: The traveller returned from the leechy swamp.

PIPKIN *howls.*

PIPKIN: The lights are on in Downing Street. I'll be revenged, I'll be big! I'll open a lady's hairdressers and burn off their hair. No I won't. I'll be a prostitute, seduce a Cabinet Minister's daughter and blackmail Thatcher!

ARTHUR: Pipkin, mate –

PIPKIN: I've been close to Margaret Thatcher as I am to you. She's so small, her skin's so clear, her teeth are wet, I'm going to kill myself.

MILLY (*aside*): I wonder when Geoffrey Howe's going to kill himself? The Cambridge Economics Group: four-and-a-half million unemployed by 1985. Output falling every year. The first time that's happened in Britain for one hundred and ten years. Get out the razor, Geoffrey.

ARTHUR (*aside*): That's what we ought to learn from Japan. Not robots. People dis-

embowelling 'emselves, from shame.

PIPKIN: I'll bomb her! I'll die a hero! I'll be an anarchist!

ARTHUR: Anarchist? Sort of far to the left of the far right of the Tory Party? Oh very well done.

PIPKIN: I'm on my own. I'm in terror.

MILLY: Thatcher's philosophy, Pipkin. Don't mind the pit, you dug it.

PIPKIN: I wish I was an animal. I wish I was mould, growing quietly in a milk bottle. Without a mind.

Tell me what to do!

A crash. The OLD MAN *strides on with* JEAN, *the baby in her arms.*

OLD MAN: What is this? Bourgeois despair? Enough of this enlightened self-disgust!

He hits PIPKIN *with his stick.*

PIPKIN: Ow!

OLD MAN: Worm talk! To the worm the nails on the boot look like stars.

JEAN: This is me Grandpa. He's come to cheer you up.

PIPKIN: He's a loony. He's a left-wing Mary Whitehouse. He's mad.

OLD MAN: Inspired!

He hits PIPKIN *again.*

JEAN: I thought you'd like to meet him. He wants to do you over.

The OLD MAN *points the stick at* ARTHUR.

OLD MAN: What is that creature?

JEAN: Mr Arthur Stacker. He's in the Ecology Party.

OLD MAN: Does that explain his condition?

MILLY: He has just rejoined the CP.

OLD MAN: That does explain his condition.

ARTHUR: Here am I, a born-again Stalinist of three minutes standing. Up pops a wally with a beard come to tell me I *still* got it wrong –

JEAN: He insulted you, Arthur. Go on. Have a row.

MILLY: I know you. Bible-belt socialist are you dear? Knocking off policemen's helmets with William Blake?

JEAN: Milly believes in the Labour Party.

OLD MAN: Reformist! You sheep in wolf's clothing. Is this the state of the Left today? Geriatrics with tubes in their arms. Overgrown children spewing bile.

(*At* MILLY:) And you – soaking endless agendas with your vital fluids, paddling water on committees till you drown.

MILLY: Tactics, you old bag of bones!

OLD MAN: Principles, you wizened hag!

PIPKIN (*to* JEAN): He nearly broke my arm!

ARTHUR: That's dialectics for you, Pipkin.

MILLY: What has Thatcher got? Votes. The police. Army. Press. TV. Tax collectors. In the end, prison. What has the Left got? The agendas, the committees – scrupulous democracy.

OLD MAN: More, Mrs Stacker. The iron force of reason. And the belief that man is not evil.

MILLY: Preachy!

OLD MAN: I'm a preacher.

MILLY: You a saint then?

OLD MAN: No, a monster! Ha!

Strikes the floor.

Storm Mammon's gate.

MILLY: I am. I'm pushing Wedgie Benn.

ARTHUR: Oh dear oh dear –

MILLY: Don't knock democracy. Got the run-down bugger, use it –

ARTHUR: Don't listen to her, she thinks she knows the answers. Now I *do* know the answers. Internationalism, beloved. Money owns half the world – we've already nabbed the other half! I mean I know there's two or three things wrong with Bulgaria –

OLD MAN: Sort it out! Our young men's hands are cut off. Give them golden fists. Hurry! And where's my tea?

JEAN: Oh I love you, you stupid old visionary bastard. Do come down to the ground. What do you want? The Archangel Gabriel beheading Tory Ministers in Parliament Square?

OLD MAN: Insurrection. Now.

JEAN: They'd put our bones under the motorways. You've seen That Woman's England. Need a real Party, Grandad. With street maps and sledgehammers and guns.

MILLY: !

PIPKIN: Parties? Parties? I know! I'll join the lot!

OLD MAN: Liberal!

The OLD MAN *waves his stick.* PIPKIN *collapses.*

PIPKIN: I want a divorce.

JEAN: You can't have a divorce, Pipkin.

PIPKIN *wilts.*

This is the mad Socialist extended family. And you're stuck in it.

MILLY: You'll get used to it Pipkin! You'll get old, bashed. You'll wonder what's going to pop first. Liver? Kidneys? Belief? Your hands will go like claws. But what'll you say?

ARTHUR: Sod defeat.

MILLY: Oh Jean, I haven't had an evening of faith for years.

OLD MAN: Evening of reason!

MILLY: Of reasonable faith?

OLD MAN: No. Comrades must never agree. How can we all get on with each other if we do that?

JEAN: One thing to thank Thatcher for. She's ended the thirty-year con – 'consensus politics'. She's taken her mask off.

OLD MAN: We will now have the argument of our lives. By breakfast we will have done. Begin.

They all rush off, arguing. But for the OLD MAN, *who follows a step behind.*

Scene Six

5 a.m. MARGARET's *sitting-room.*
KEITH *and* GEOFFREY *are with her.*
KEITH *is hammering his hand to the floor
with a six inch-nail. The* GHOST OF
AIREY NEAVE *lurks in the shadows.*

GEOFFREY (*sucking* MILTON's *coca
cola bottle*): The CBI have locked themselves in Centre Point. They're up to
something in the lift shaft.

He wails.

Monetarism is on the run. I stare at my
stool in the lavatory pan for signs of
something going right. What are we going
to do?

MARGARET: Isn't it wonderful the way
the Pope says things.

GEOFFREY: What?

MARGARET: Perhaps he could say
something for Britain from his window.

A silence.

GEOFFREY: What?

MARGARET: He hates Russia too.

NEAVE (*a whisper*): Margaret – Margaret
– The dead have sent me. Can't you hear
me –

GEOFFREY: My thinking is so thin! I can
hardly add up!

MARGARET: Isn't that an impediment in
your line of work?

KEITH: Aaaaaaaaargh!

MARGARET (*calmly*): Yes Keith?

KEITH: There *is* another society we can
model ourselves on.

MARGARET: Not Russia –

KEITH: Hong Kong.

MARGARET: Don't they – I mean, on
their boats –

GEOFFREY: Junks, Margaret –

MARGARET: Aren't there a lot of rats?

GEOFFREY: Babies born in buckets.
Sewage in your gin. Utter squalor, I
would guess.

MARGARET: I've not seen much squalor.
And I went to Oxford.

Touching GEOFFREY *on the arm.*

We mustn't think about horrible things
too much, Geoffrey. We mustn't weaken.

NEAVE (*a whisper*): Margaret –
Margaret –

KEITH: They do live in squalor! There are
cataracts in their eyes! But they're free!

Banging the nail.

Free in the sweat shops. Free to suffer.

MARGARET: How true Keith. We must
be cruel.

GEOFFREY: To be kind.

MARGARET: I wouldn't go that far.

GEOFFREY: Trouble is, there's an awful
lot of 'em out there –

MARGARET: Don't bend, Geoffrey. I
will never bend. I must lend you my big
sunglasses. I had them made for me when
I went to visit the black people in Lusaka.
I knew, you see. They'd want to throw
acid in my face.

GEOFFREY: You're a brick, Margaret.

KEITH: We do not know the secret of
growth or how to generate it.

Banging the nail.

There is nothing we can do.

Banging the nail.

Just throw the people back into the stone
age. Whoever re-invents the telephone,
he is master.

GEOFFREY: What does he mean? I wish I
was a genius.

MARGARET: Keith means, if industry
isn't profitable, doesn't thrive, we close
the country down. Let people protest in
the streets, let them strike for months, let
their factories fall apart. We have friends
abroad who will support us. People are
very cheap. Let them suffer.

GEOFFREY: Three years?

KEITH: Ten years?

MARGARET: I don't think Chile's such a
bad place. The CBI like it too. Their
report was very encouraging. They say in
Santiago people sit in cafés and look very
well dressed. I'm so glad I sent my
Ambassador back.

GEOFFREY: Torture nuns there, don't they –

MARGARET: Who can you trust these days? And if you're going to be free we need a big police force to help my lovely big boys in the SAS to kill people.

WILLY *crawls through with a body.*

GEOFFREY: I feel I'm underground. The bunker.

WILLIE: People in the streets. Black bags of garbage. I know, my policemen tell me. Gimme whitewash, Margaret. Slosh over a lot. I tell the people, stay in your homes. Let the police walk the streets in peace.

NEAVE (*a whisper*): Margaret – it's me – Airey.

MARGARET: If Airey were here, I wonder what he'd say?

NEAVE (*a whisper*): Margaret. The dead are communists!

She takes out a small silver casket from her handbag.

GEOFFREY: For godsake, what have you got there? It looks like ashes.

MARGARET: Just a little bit of Airey.

NEAVE: No. No. The soul is socialist.

KEITH: Squalor! Old age! We must not see them – it would not be kind! Let's tear out our eyes –

He tears at his eyes with his free hand.

MARGARET: You take things so personally, Keith. It's morning. Geoffrey – close the curtains.

She opens the casket. Dips the tip of her finger in and touches it to the tip of her tongue.

(*Aside.*) You had a word of comfort from me. Now here is a word of advice.

Don't do anything silly. Go home and hang yourselves if you like. I know some of you are Socialist, but you will never hang me.

And you know, if the bomb does go off while you're on the tube tonight, put a paper bag over your head.

And you know, if you do get home, lock the door.

And you know, though I be small-minded, ignorant, and the ruin of you, you will vote for me in 1984.

Or the British will have to make Socialism work. And you daren't, dare you?

She points at her buttocks.

Kiss!